WORLD CHESS CHAMPIONSHIP

KASPAROV
v
SHORT

DANIEL KING and DONALD TRELFORD

LONDON, NEW YORK

Cadogan Books
Distribution

UK/EUROPE/AUSTRALASIA/ASIA/AFRICA
Distribution: Grantham Book Services Ltd, Isaac Newton Way,
Alma Park Industrial Estate, Grantham, Lincs NG31 9SD.
Tel: 0476 67421; Fax: 0476 590223.

USA/CANADA/LATIN AMERICA/JAPAN
Distribution: Macmillan Distribution Center, Front & Brown
Streets, Riverside, New Jersey 08075, USA.
Tel: (609) 461 6500; Fax: (609) 764 9122.

First published 1993

British Library Cataloguing-in-Publication Data
A CIP catalogue record for this book is available from the British Library.

ISBN 1 85744 0668

Cover photo by Fabio Biagi.

Edited by Andrew Kinsman.

Typeset by ChessSetter.

Printed in Great Britain by Redwood Books, Trowbridge, Wilts

Contents

About this book

World Chess Championship is the story of the Kasparov-Short match which took place in London in September/October 1993. For those interested in which author was responsible for which sections, Donald Trelford wrote the introduction and background to each game, whilst Daniel King was responsible for the game annotations. In the text the division is clearly indicated by the use of a single-column layout for Donald Trelford's material and double-column for Daniel King's.

The notation used to record the chess moves in this book is known as 'figurine algebraic notation'. For those unfamiliar with chess notation, or perhaps acquainted only with the older 'English descriptive notation', there follows a brief explanation.

Each square of the chessboard has a co-ordinate, working on a very similar principle to an A-Z road atlas. Thus the square on the bottom left hand side is known as 'a1' and the square on the top right as 'h8'. Every other square on the board also has a unique co-ordinate as shown by the diagram. The pieces themselves are indicated by figurines of the individual pieces. Thus on the first move White might perhaps play 1 ♘f3. No figurines are used to denote pawn moves, so 1...d5 would be a pawn move for Black.

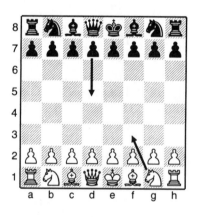

Other symbols and abbreviations

0-0	Castles kingside
0-0-0	Castles queenside
x	Captures
+	Check
!	Good move
!!	Brilliant move
?	Bad move
??	Blunder
!?	Interesting move
?!	Dubious move
(D)	Diagram follows

Introduction

The British challenge

Of the 13 world chess champions since the title was formally introduced in 1886, not one had come from Britain. Before Nigel Short, no Briton had even challenged for the crown. Short's challenge was therefore a unique and historic aspect of *The Times* world chess championship of 1993, and concentrated an unprecedented public and media spotlight on the event and on the game of chess, especially in this country.

It was also the first championship for more than 40 years to be contested outside the aegis of the world chess body FIDE (Federation Internationale des Echecs), the two players having broken away to form a new Professional Chess Association of their own. British players and chess organisations were divided over this move, which meant that the challenger received less patriotic support than he might otherwise have expected. This caused a certain bitterness to surround the event.

To add to the general air of controversy, FIDE arranged a rival match, which they also called 'the world championship', between the Russian former champion, Anatoly Karpov, and the Dutchman Jan Timman, both of whom had been beaten by Short on his way to the final. This began in Holland the day before the London match, but ran into repeated difficulties over sponsorship.

Commercial support for the Short-Kasparov encounter, though drummed up in haste after the break with FIDE, was not such a problem. *The Times*, part of Rupert Murdoch's world-wide media empire, put up a prize fund of £1.7 million, five-eighths of which would go to the winner, as well as massive promotional spending to stage the event and acres of space in the newspaper itself. *The Times* used the occasion to cut its price by 50 per cent to 30p on the day before the match in an aggressive marketing gambit against its rivals.

A co-sponsor was Channel 4, which had exclusive rights to live film of the match and gave extensive coverage in a popular format, with inventive use of graphics, designed to make chess more accessible to the general public. The programme was fronted by Carol Vorderman and featured Grandmasters Raymond Keene, Jon Speelman and Daniel King. Channel 4 also had exclusive interviews with the players after the game.

In response, BBC2 put out an evening programme, chaired by News-night presenters Peter Snow and Francine Stock, with comment by William Hartston and Dominic Lawson, editor of *The Spectator* and a close friend of Short's, who were later to fall out in public over the match. The BBC, in contrast to Channel 4, set out to unravel the intricacies of the game like the politics of Bosnia or the Middle East. Between them the two channels provided nine hours of coverage a week, more than had ever been devoted to chess before. It was seen as a test of the game's mass appeal.

Teleworld Holding BV, a media technology group based in Rotterdam, were early sponsors of the event, and their requirements for a Predict-a-Move competition determined the form of the match – a total of 24 games, to be played on three days a week (Tuesday, Thursday and Saturday) between 7 September and 30 October. It was agreed that all the games would be played out, irrespective of the state of the match. By the time the company withdrew its sponsorship, this format had been set and could only be changed by agreement between all parties.

For Garry Kasparov, champion since 1985, it was his sixth world championship match, but his first against any other opponent than Karpov. Asked at an earlier stage who would be his challenger, the Russian grandmaster had said: 'It will be Short and it will be short.' For his part, Short had said of the champion: 'He is a very nasty guy. The sooner he gets beaten the better.' In such a spirit, alas, are world chess championships invariably played.

The world title

Until 1886, there was no official world champion, though various players had dominated the chess of their time. The Frenchman, Philidor, was widely acknowledged as supreme in the eighteenth century, followed by two of his fellow countrymen, Deschapelles and La Bourdonnais. An Irishman, Alexander McDonnell, played a long series of games against La Bourdonnais in 1834, all recorded for posterity, in which the Frenchman had the advantage.

Then came Howard Staunton, the greatest British player of the nineteenth century, who sponsored the standard chess pieces used today. He established his ascendancy in a famous victory over the Frenchman, Pierre St Amant, in Paris in 1843, but then became too ill for a return match.

The world championship of 1993 coincided with the 150th anniversary of Staunton's historic Paris victory, which brought the chess crown over the Channel for the first time. Leading British players and officials wrote to *The Times* on the opening day of the match to seek some permanent commemoration in Britain of Staunton's contribution to the game.

One of his most important contributions to the game was to organise the first international chess tournament at the Great Exhibition in London in 1851. This was won by the German master, Adolf Anderssen, who went on to play several famous challenge matches, losing finally to the eccentric American genius, Paul Morphy.

Morphy, who was to spend the last two decades of his life in a state of clinical depression, was a young prodigy and dominated the chess of his age. He died two years before the official world championship came into being in 1886.

The first man to claim the official title of world chess champion was Wilhelm Steinitz, who defeated his great German rival, Johannes Zukertort, at St Louis. Steinitz, who had been born in Prague and lived in Vienna, died penniless in a New York lunatic asylum in 1900, having surrendered his title to another German, Emanuel Lasker, six years before.

Lasker reigned for longer than any world champion in history until he was beaten by the Cuban genius, José Raoul Capablanca, in 1921. In those days there was no formal procedure for defending the world title and champions naturally hung on for as long as they could, creating difficulties over the date, the venue or the prize fund before putting their titles at risk. Bobby Fischer was by no means the first chess champion to create such problems over the terms on which a challenge match would be played.

Capablanca was toppled six years later by the white Russian émigré, Alexander Alekhine, Kasparov's favourite player, who held the title, with one brief interruption, for the next two decades. The interruption came from a Dutchman, Max Euwe, who beat the Russian in 1935, allegedly while he was the worse for drink, but conceded the crown in a return match two years later.

When Alekhine died after the war, the championship was settled at a tournament split between The Hague and Moscow in 1948, won by the Soviet player Botvinnik, who in the next 15 years lost and regained the title twice from his fellow countrymen, Smyslov and Tal, before losing to another, Tigran Petrosian, in 1963. The crafty Armenian, a great defensive tactician, was beaten in turn by Boris Spassky, who lost the most contentious and highly publicised chess challenge of all time to the eccentric American genius, Bobby Fischer, at Reykjavik in 1972.

When Fischer persistently refused to agree on terms for a defence of his title, FIDE named Anatoly Karpov as champion in 1975. The Russian established his credentials with two bitterly fought victories over the defector, Victor Korchnoi, and remained champion for a decade until he was unseated after two marathon battles by Garry Kasparov.

The full list of world champions is as follows:

1886	Wilhelm Steinitz
1894	Emanuel Lasker
1921	José Raoul Capablanca
1927	Alexander Alekhine
1935	Max Euwe
1937	Alekhine
1948	Mikhail Botvinnik
1957	Vassily Smyslov
1958	Botvinnik
1960	Mikhail Tal
1961	Botvinnik
1963	Tigran Petrosian
1969	Boris Spassky
1972	Bobby Fischer
1975	Anatoly Karpov
1985	Garry Kasparov

The champion

Garry Kasparov was born in Baku in Azerbaijan, on the shores of the Caspian Sea, on 13 April 1963. His father, Kim Weinstein, was a Jewish engineer in the Caspian oilfields who had died of cancer when his son was seven, but not before he had taught him the moves in chess. They were a family of musicians. His mother, Clara, was an Armenian engineer/electrician who worked for a research institute until she gave it up to support her son's career. The young Weinstein, brought up with a family of Kasparovs, adopted their name in his teens.

His talent for chess took him first to the Pioneers' Palace in Baku, named after the Soviet cosmonaut Yuri Gagarin, and then, by the age of ten, to the Botvinnik school, named after the former world champion. In 1975, when he was still only 12, he made such an impression at the USSR junior championship at Vilnius that the *Guardian's* chess correspondent, Leonard Barden, wrote: 'In my opinion there is a very clear favourite for world champion in 1990. He is Garry Weinstein, from Baku.' Barden's prediction turned out to be five years late, but it was remarkable nonetheless.

Chess players have a natural affinity for mathematics, but Kasparov's mother, herself a powerful and attractive personality who had devoted herself to her only child's future after her husband's early death, insisted that Garry should be taught languages and literature to give him a more rounded education.

At 17, Garry won the world junior championship at Dortmund, just one and a half points ahead of a certain Nigel Short, who was to say later: 'I have never faced such an intense player, never felt such energy and concentration, such will and desire burning across the board towards me.' Although 13 years were to pass before they finally met in the world championship, Kasparov always remembered this early encounter and sensed that the bespectacled Englishman would one day be his challenger.

For the next four years Kasparov was engaged in a hidden battle with the Soviet bureaucracy for the right to challenge Karpov, who had become the court favourite with his Cold War victories over Victor Korchnoi. Kasparov was prevented by various forms of red tape from playing in the overseas tournaments he needed to broaden his experience. When he asked Nikolai Krogius, a member of the Soviet sports committee, why his progress was being blocked, he was told: 'At the moment we have a world champion and we don't need another.'

In contrast to Karpov, Kasparov was seen as a potential threat to Soviet orthodoxy, an individualist southern rebel, half-Jewish, half-Armenian, who appeared to adapt too easily to Western style and manners and might therefore, they feared, choose to become another defector like Korchnoi.

When Kasparov finally won his opportunity to challenge Karpov in 1984, having defeated Korchnoi and the former world champion Smyslov in the eliminating rounds, he still suspected that the Soviet authorities were against him. His worst fears were confirmed in the match itself. Having gone four and then five games down in Moscow, he fought back through a long series of draws in an historic rearguard action that took Karpov to the brink of a nervous breakdown. With the score standing at 5-3 to Karpov FIDE intervened, with the support of the Soviet chess authorities, to abandon the match.

Kasparov's epic dispute with FIDE and its Filipino president, Florencio Campomanes, dates from this time. He suspected FIDE of colluding with the Soviet Chess Federation to keep Karpov on the world throne. The dispute culminated in the breakaway by Short and himself to stage their own world championship event in London in 1993.

Kasparov finally beat Karpov in the re-match in Moscow in 1985 to become the youngest world champion at the age of 22, and then defended the title against him three times over the next five years, becoming in the process the highest rated player in the history of the game. There have since been indications, supported by former KGB officials, that the Soviet chess authorities tried to bribe Kasparov's seconds to betray his opening plans.

It was through the personal frustrations he suffered in his career that Kasparov came to have doubts about the Soviet system and to put his trust in the early Gorbachev reforms. Only later did he come to realise that the Soviet Communist system itself was incorrigible and that democracy held out the only hope for his countrymen.

In the run-up to the world championship Nigel Short accused Kasparov of remaining an old Soviet Communist at heart. This charge was way off the mark and also remarkably insensitive – a lapse only to be explained by the fact that Short was listening too closely to his fiercely anti-Soviet trainer, Lubomir Kavalek, who had escaped to the United States from Czechoslovakia after the 'Prague Spring' of 1968. 'Lubosh', a peppery character, was to disappear there again after only a few games of the London match.

Kasparov, as I know personally from writing a book with him during the Gorbachev years, is a genuine democrat who put his own life and reputation at risk in the anti-Armenian pogrom in his native Baku in 1989, when he hired a plane at his own expense to fly out refugees from the 'ethnic cleansing' by Azeris. He has never returned to his home region since.

He sees Boris Yeltsin as a powerful and essential transitional figure between the old Soviet system and genuine Russian democracy. Yeltsin's bloody showdown with the Russian Parliament took place during the London match. Kasparov kept in close touch with events by telephone from his Regent's Park headquarters and through CNN and the BBC. He never wavered in his belief that the Russian leader was on top of events and pursuing the right policy.

What can be fairly said about the Russian grandmaster however, is that he is probably the last great product of the Soviet chess machine, a player who has been subsidised and trained at the state's expense from an early age, an advantage denied to his western rivals. His chess coaches, his fitness trainers, and the travel and living expenses of himself and his family, all came from the Soviet state.

After an early, much-publicised dalliance with a famous and much older actress, Kasparov has now settled down to marriage with a translator, Maria ('Masha'), with whom he has a daughter. Although they have a flat in central Moscow, Maria lives mostly in Helsinki with her Russian parents while her husband is globetrotting. He earns vast sums playing exhibitions in places like South America, as well as endorsing computers and clothing.

He has been greatly assisted in these commercial activities, as well as in his chess career, by his friend and business manager for many years, Andrew Page, an Englishman who was formerly an actor and racing driver. They have developed a mutually beneficial business partnership, the Muscovy Company, that is well placed to profit from the thaw in Russia's relations with the West.

Even without the support of the Communist system, Kasparov still manages to maintain a substantial apparatus to provide the backing for his chess. For the London match his chess coaches were the Russian grandmasters Belyavsky, Azmaiparashvili and Makarychev, with Shakharov to look after his computer database. He also had two fitness trainers who doubled as bodyguards, as well as his mother to supervise the kitchen.

Kasparov has always believed in diet control and exercise to build up the physical stamina needed for the many hours of concentration required at the chessboard. He goes cycling, jogging, plays football and lifts weights in the gym. Even Short, not a notably athletic figure, went swimming every day as he prepared for the match.

As he began his fourth title defence, the only questions hung over the champion's personal commitment, given the worrying upheavals in Russia, his long period at the top, and the psychological effect of the breakaway from FIDE. His friends were also concerned that he might not take the British challenge with quite the seriousness it seemed to deserve, since he could not, in his heart of hearts, really believe that Short could ever beat him.

Kasparov's career record in summary:

1975   USSR junior champion (aged 12).
1979   Wins first international tournament at Banja Luka.
1980   World junior champion. Grandmaster.
1982   Qualifies for world championship cycle.
1984   Challenges Karpov for the world title.
1985   Match abandoned. Wins re-match to become youngest world champion at 22.

1986   Successfully defends title against Karpov in Leningrad and
       London.
1987   Ties with Karpov in Seville, retaining title.
1990   Beats Karpov in New York and Lyons.
1993   Defends title against first British challenger, Nigel Short.

The challenger

At 28, Nigel Short is only two years younger than the champion,
though he strikes outsiders as much less mature. This is partly physical, Kasparov seeming much older in his appearance and general demeanour, but the differences go beyond that. Both are married with
baby daughters.

Short's National Health-style glasses, spiky hair and general air of
gawkiness have led to him being described as resembling 'a computer
nerd who has accidentally hacked into the Pentagon'. Though doubtless unfair, this image is not helped by the challenger's precise, rather
strangulated mode of address. Compared with the sleek, cosmopolitan
Kasparov, with his silk suits and male model chic, Short comes over
like a spotty adolescent. When the two speak at a press conference together, the polished and voluble Russian outperforms the hesitant,
stammering Englishman in his own language.

Short has gained in confidence since marrying his Greek-born wife,
Rea, a psychoanalyst who is seven years his senior, and through his association with Kavalek. The expenses of the coach were met by a commercial sponsor, Eagle Star.

Rea's influence may be gauged from an incident witnessed by Short's
friend and confidant, Dominic Lawson, during the semi-final against
Timman. Short was depressed at losing a vital game that had lasted
eight hours. Rea fixed her husband with a glare: 'I will give you the advice my Spartan countrywomen gave their men as they left for battle.
Come back either with your shield or upon it!'. Short gulped, then went
out and won.

He was born at Leigh in Lancashire. The family crossed the Penni-
nes to Sheffield, then returned to Atherton, following his father's job,
first in journalism, then in public relations. Nigel is the second of three
brothers. The parents divorced when the boys were in their teens.

Nigel was not outstanding at school, apparently playing down his
natural cleverness, and earned brief notoriety by playing the bass
guitar with a punk group called 'The Urge'. Although his chess talent
was discovered while he was very young, he did not apply himself to

developing it with the same single-minded dedication that Kasparov and other Russian prodigies were encouraged to do.

Until he suffered a serious professional reverse in 1988, losing to his fellow British grandmaster, Jon Speelman, in a world championship eliminator, he seemed to be coasting on his talent, relying on his remarkable positional flair and instinct rather than working at the detailed chores of chess analysis.

Kavalek brought a more rigorous professionalism to his chess preparations, as well as a killer instinct. For the championship, Short also had the help of Speelman and of Robert Hübner, Germany's leading grandmaster, an expert in Egyptian hieroglyphics, which led one writer to speculate that he had been brought in because he could answer the riddle of the Sphinx.

Short entered the match with a patchy tournament record and a relatively low world rating, but he had proved his competitive strength as the first Briton in history to mount a challenge for the world crown. This made him not only the leading home player since Howard Staunton, but also the country's first chess millionaire.

Nonetheless, he did not command the full backing of Britain's leading players and officials, who believed he had sacrificed his integrity in breaking away from the game's governing body simply, as they saw it, to make more money for himself. Short is candid in responding to this charge: 'Maybe it's not very noble, but I have decided that the best way I can promote chess in Britain is if I become world champion and look after my own interests.'

Short's overriding problem, however, was a fatal lack of confidence when confronted by Kasparov's formidable record – a weakness he countered by bluster on the eve of the match, charging the champion with all sorts of character defects. 'Garry Kasparov was not spanked enough as a child,' he claimed. 'He surrounds himself with people who are almost his slaves ... As a player he indulges in unethical behaviour. It is pure intimidation.'

Kasparov proudly refused to rise to these allegations in the pre-match banter. He was saving his spanking for the chessboard.

Short's career record in summary:

1977   Youngest player (12) to qualify for British championship, where he defeats Jonathan Penrose, ten-times British champion.

1979   Misses British title on tie-break.

1980   Awarded International Master title.

1984   Britain's youngest-ever grandmaster, wins British championship.
1985   Qualifies as Britain's first-ever world championship candidate.
1987   Qualifies again as world championship candidate, regains British title.
1988   Loses to Speelman in world championship quarter-final.
1991   Reaches world championship semi-final.
1992   Defeats former world champion Karpov.
1993   Beats Timman for right to challenge Kasparov.

The breakaway

Kasparov's distrust of FIDE goes back to 1985, when his first challenge for the world title was abandoned in circumstances that have never been fully explained. More than once after that he had tried to break away from the world body, or to have Campomanes overthrown, but he had failed to persuade his fellow grandmasters to join him in a *putsch*.

When the arrangements were announced by FIDE for the 1993 world championship, the Russian had at first gone along with the choice of Manchester, then still bidding for the Olympic Games in 2000 AD, who had offered a prize fund of £1.1 million. Short, however, was out of contact in Greece at the time and claims that FIDE never consulted him about the bid.

He rang Kasparov in outrage, claiming not only that he had been insulted by the failure to consult, but that the financial proposals could be bettered. It may have been in his mind that Bobby Fischer had been promised a much higher sum by a Yugoslav banker for his re-match with Boris Spassky in 1992 (though the banker appears to have fled before all the money was paid). Kasparov had doubts as to whether more sponsorship money could in fact be raised in a period of recession, but he could hardly ignore such a call to arms.

Here was the chance he had been waiting for. At last the world's two leading players had it in their power to cock a snook at FIDE. This could never have happened with Karpov, who appeared to be in league with Campomanes, or with the chess bureaucracy of the former Soviet Union. Now, if the players could organise their own world championship without the services of FIDE, it would be a devastating blow on behalf of player power. But how could they raise the money?

It was here that Raymond Keene, the British grandmaster and chess correspondent of *The Times*, made a decisive intervention. He persuaded the Murdoch group to put up the money and he persuaded the players to accept it. A bonus was that the players did not have to pay FIDE its usual 25 per cent commission out of the prize fund.

FIDE did not take these developments lying down. They decided that Kasparov and Short had expelled themselves from the world championship, so stripped them of their international chess ratings and called on Timman and Karpov to play for the 'vacant' world title. The stage – indeed *two* stages – were thus set for a showdown over the whole future control of international chess.

The arena

In London the stage was that of the Savoy Theatre, which had recently been restored after a fire in 1990. Originally the home of the D'Oyle Carte operas, it had opened in 1881, eight years ahead of the hotel itself, with a production of 'Patience' by Gilbert and Sullivan. This had been launched with an added attraction – the first electric light in a public building in the capital.

A few doors along was the famous restaurant, Simpson's-in-the-Strand, now also part of the Savoy group, which had been a popular gathering place for chess players in the nineteenth century. For the price of a shilling a Victorian gentleman could approach the famous Divan and smoke a cigar and enjoy a game of chess.

It was in this historic and welcoming environment that the draw for the match took place, and where the media and the world's grandmasters made their headquarters. On the opening day of the match, 7 September, *The Times* declared in a rousing editorial: 'London is once again the capital of world chess.'

The paper thundered on: 'There is a big idea behind this match: it is freedom from Cold War bureaucracy, freedom for individuals to compete for proper rewards, the democratic freedom that comes from maximising the advantages of modern communications to popularise the game. Whoever wins the Kasparov-Short match, this liberation of world chess will continue.'

Other commentators were not so sanguine. The *Spectator* caught a rather different mood in a signed piece by Dominic Lawson headlined 'Fear and Loathing at the Savoy'.

Game 1

Kasparov-Short
Ruy Lopez, Anti-Marshall

The crowds outside the gleaming chrome entrance to the Savoy Theatre might have been queuing up for its usual dramatic repertoire, except that not enough of them were female. They were also talking excitedly about chess, even guessing at the likely opening moves. 'Will it be a King's Indian, a Queen's Gambit or just a Nimzo-Indian?' I heard someone say to his companion. Some had travelled by train from outside London, if not with extravagant hopes of a British triumph, at least to see their man put up a good show, catch a glimpse of the legendary Kasparov and say they'd been present at this historic event.

The realists were estimating how far Nigel Short would get before Kasparov reached the 12 points he needed to retain his title. 'It will be 12-6', said one spectator firmly. 'No, it will be closer than that, you'll see', said his friend. I found only one man in the queue, an air traffic controller from Gatwick, who believed the British challenger could possibly win.

Because of an extended security search, the audience were not let into the theatre until just before the opening, which meant that they overflowed the pavement by the Savoy taxi rank as television cameras buzzed among them. The busy scene puzzled the more smartly dressed clientele leaving the hotel after a good lunch, who wondered what was going on. One of these diners was David Mellor, the former Minister, who was immediately pursued by the microphones and asked about the chess. 'I'm a great fan of Short's,' he said crisply, unsurprised by the media attention, 'especially now that he's no longer SDP and is a Tory.'

Andrew Page, Kasparov's manager, appeared with his wife and son. 'Garry's in good shape, quietly confident', he said in the tones of a football manager sitting on top of the league. Richard Doubleday, from the Central Council of Physical Recreation, said he was 'in raptures' at the thought of seeing the chess. John Beveridge, a distinguished QC, also confessed to an addiction to the game.

The newly restored Art Deco theatre was nearly full, despite gloomy predictions, though how many had been packed in by the sponsors to fill the seats, as had been wickedly rumoured, was anybody's guess.

The price of seats had been reduced and special offers made through the Murdoch papers, including (improbably) to readers of the *Sun*, where Nigel had been portrayed across a double-page spread as a punk guitarist, chess's answer to Nigel Kennedy. I had no difficulty buying a seat at the box office, so it couldn't have been a sell-out.

Chess books and all kinds of souvenirs, including T-shirts, were on sale in the theatre bars. The first thing the audience had to master once they'd found their seats was the technology to make the head-sets work, so that they could hear a running commentary by grandmasters to find out what was going on.

The stage set included a giant knight on an angle and illuminated chessboards on the wall by each player, with a flashing light to show the latest move. The players had had their first disagreement about the seats. Short had chosen a red leather carver, very upright, in keeping with his stiffer personality – as somebody said, it was the sort of furniture you might expect to see in a Terence Rattigan revival. Kasparov had a lower, racier, more modern affair in black leather and chrome. When the curtain rose on the action, however, Short's chair was green, the one originally intended for Kasparov. A stagehand appeared to make a swift substitution. On such questions of detail have previous world championships foundered.

After a welcoming speech by Raymond Keene, the British grandmaster who had done so much to bring the match to the Savoy, the editor of his paper, *The Times*, Peter Stothard, which had committed so much money to the event, made Kasparov's first move for him to mark the formal opening, pawn to e4. Kasparov's last defence in London, against Karpov in 1986, had been opened by Margaret Thatcher, but she had kept her hands off the chessboard.

The head-set commentary was good, surprisingly jolly and relatively easy for follow, even for non-chess experts. Without it, in fact, it was hard to tell who was winning, as the giant display boards blinked away without revealing any clues. Unfortunately, some studio laughter spilled out of the head-sets into the air round the players, who both looked up crossly to trace the source of this irreverent and unmannerly breach of their concentration. Had they listened more carefully, they would have heard their next moves being predicted by the experts.

Both players kept going off-stage between moves to their rest-rooms, where they could keep in touch with the chessboard through monitor screens, but were not allowed to talk to anyone. Like everything else, the refreshments had been carefully prepared to meet each player's requirements. Kasparov prefers chocolate, washed down by mineral or tonic water. Short, too, likes chocolate, but insists that it has to be Swiss. He also has sandwiches, but no ham.

On-stage, in addition to the players, were the two arbiters, Yuri Averbakh and Carlos Falcon, sitting silently at their table, and the Channel 4 cameras, shrouded in black cloth. The TV studio was right behind the stage, amid the crowded warren of winding stairs that constitutes the backstage world of the theatre.

In *The Times* Daniel Johnson described Short as 'that rare figure: a British hero. Silent, lost in thought, he may not look like a man of destiny.' That was certainly true. 'The world champion,' he added, 'looked as elegant, intense and sexually magnetic as ever. More than one female has expressed curiosity about the hairy body about which Short seems to know.'

This was a reference to a bizarre interview Short had given to a German magazine, *Sports*, in which he had said of the Russian: 'He sometimes behaves like a primate. He runs around like a gorilla. Just look at him, he's covered from head to foot with hair.'

Meanwhile, back at the chessboard, the situation was not looking hairy for either player. The experts – whether heard through the headsets in the theatre, in the Grandmasters' room in the basement of the nearby restaurant, Simpson's-in-the-Strand, or in the ornate, high-ceilinged press room two floors up – were agreed that the game seemed to be heading towards a draw as the players scrambled to complete their 40 moves in two hours.

Although both were clearly rushed, it came as a total surprise when the arbiters solemnly approached the table to confer with the players. It was clear that something unexpected had happened. Some people thought Kasparov had lost, but then it became sickeningly clear that it was Short's flag that had fallen dramatically, his hand trembling and failing to make the time control.

It was the worst possible start to what was bound to be a long and gruelling ordeal. British grandmasters, especially Tony Miles, could barely contain their contempt for their colleague's unprofessional lapse. 'Pure panic,' said one, 'there's no possible excuse. He mismanaged his clock completely.' Another said grimly: 'Kasparov didn't win it, Short lost it.' Speelman, who was helping Short's preparations, said later: 'It was a disgusting way to lose.'

Here is Daniel King's commentary on the first game of the match.

In a scene reminiscent of a boxing world title fight, the two contestants were heralded on stage by *The Times* chess correspondent, Raymond Keene. First, the challenger Nigel Short from stage right, to thunderous applause and a blitz of camera flashes; followed by the world champion Garry Kasparov from stage left. The players shook hands in a manner which might even be described as friendly—there was little evidence of the eyeballing and crushing handshakes which Kasparov and Karpov used to indulge in as part of the pre-game ritual. Peter Stothard, the editor of *The Times*, was then invited by Kasparov to play the first move of the match. After seeing the e-pawn flash forward on the giant screens behind the two players, my first thought was, did Mr Stothard hear Kasparov correctly?

1 e4

Kasparov plays 1 d4 more often than this, but on reflection it is no great surprise. He usually essays 1 e4 when he is reasonably certain as to how his opponent will reply, which is the case here.

1 ... e5

For many years Short played the French Defence almost exclusively, but when he reached the higher echelons of the chess world he began to defend the Black side of the Ruy Lopez. He once told me that he feels at his most comfortable when he has a strong point in the centre of the board (he was actually speaking about the Queen's Gambit, but the same could well apply to this move).

2 ♘f3   ♘c6
3 ♗b5

The Ruy Lopez or Spanish Opening is named after Ruy Lopez de Segura, a Spanish priest who was arguably the strongest player in Europe in the sixteenth century. Kasparov used it to score two brilliant wins against Karpov at decisive moments in their world championship matches.

3 ...   a6
4 ♗a4   ♘f6
5 0-0   ♗e7
6 ♖e1   b5
7 ♗b3   0-0

Is this bluff, or an indication of Short's aggressive mood? If Kasparov now plays 8 c3, Short may continue in classical fashion with 8...d6, or, more likely, whip out the dreaded Marshall Gambit with 8...d5; after 9 exd5 ♘xd5 10 ♘xe5 ♘xe5 11 ♖xe5 White is a pawn to the good, but has to survive a tremendous attack before he will be able to use it.

Kasparov would not have been able to predict that Short would want to go in for this, so he would naturally be at a tremendous disadvantage: it is quite possible to be mown down by home analysis in this complex and heavily analysed variation. Sensibly, he avoids a direct battle of pre-game preparation, and chooses a safer continuation. After the game he muttered darkly, 'I have discovered some information', like some Russian Cold War spy; perhaps an indication that he will now send his seconds away to do some work on the Marshall. I wonder if we will see its refutation in a later game?

8 a4

The so-called 'Anti-Marshall' prevents Black playing the dreaded gambit mentioned above. It has a reputation of being rather wimpish—running the gauntlet of the Marshall is the principled way of playing the position—and if Black plays accurately he should equalise the position without too many difficulties.

8 ...   b4

Short played this quickly, an indication that he was still in his home preparation. The most common way of dealing with the threat to the b-pawn is actually 8...♗b7, as Short himself played against Anand last year. Pushing the b-pawn is more committal— it leaves some squares on the queenside slightly weakened, in particular c4.

Kasparov sank into thought at this point. A plan is needed here rather than a specific move.

9 d3

Kasparov continues his cautious approach, playing for a slight advantage rather than trying to blast open the centre with 9 d4.

9 ...   d6

10 a5

An annoying move for Black: the b-pawn is cut off from protection by the a-pawn.

Hereabouts, Jonathan Speelman—one of Short's seconds—announced that he had had this position a couple of months ago, as White, against Vassily Smyslov in the Biel Interzonal. Our speculations as to the extent of Speelman's involvement with the preparation for this game were broken off when he confessed that he couldn't remember how his game with Smyslov had continued.

10 ...   ♗e6

A sensible move, blocking out White's dangerous bishop.

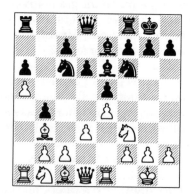

11 ♘bd2

Capturing on e6 would only strengthen Black's centre and open the f-file for a rook.

11 ...   ♖b8

Smyslov played 11...♗xb3 12 ♘xb3 in the above-mentioned

game, which hardly alters the nature of the position: Speelman was slightly better though the game ended in a draw.

12 &c4

In order to be able to move the knight on d2, which in turn blocks the bishop on c1, White must first move the bishop.

12 ...   &c8

13 &f1

The knight chugs off on its familiar Spanish route. From f1 it may leap to g3, or e3, eyeing the outposts on f5 and d5.

13 ...   &e8

Perhaps a little too routine—Short was still moving quickly. After the game Kasparov indicated the correct way for him to play: 13...&xc4! 14 dxc4 &d8!. Black manoeuvres the knight to e6 and if necessary plays ...c5 and ...&d4 to close the centre.

14 &e3   &d4?

This is a mistake. Instead, it was possible to play 14...&f8, a standard retreat, tucking the bishop out of the way of the marauding knight, with an acceptable position.

15 &xd4   exd4

16 &d5   &xd5

17 exd5

Short had foreseen this position when playing 14...&d4 and had intended 17...&g4, as he thought, virtually forcing 18 f3, and only then 18...&d7. The pawn on f3 obstructs the queen's path and therefore disrupts the smooth

flow of the rest of White's development. Unfortunately, Short had missed that after 17...&g4 White has the tactical blow 18 &xa6!, and if 18...&xd1 19 &xc8 &xc2 20 &d7 wins material.

From this moment on Kasparov assumes control.

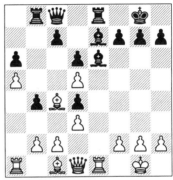

17 ...   &d7

18 &d2!   &f6

19 &xe8+   &xe8

20 &e2!

While Black's queen and rook are tied up defending the weak a- and b-pawns, White takes possession of the one open file in the position.

20 ...   &b5

21 &e1   &xc4

22 dxc4   h6

There was a threat of 23 &xb4 so the back-rank problem had to be solved.

23 b3

A tidy move, ruling out the possibility of ...d3, as well as ...b3.

23 ...   c5

Kasparov now had a critical

decision to make. Should he capture this pawn *en passant*, leaving the b-pawn weak, but freeing Black's position? In the end he chose not to, and with hindsight it can be seen that his judgement was correct: Short finds himself under enormous pressure and, what's more, has no chances for counterplay. The one weakness in Kasparov's position—the pawn on a5—is so far offside that Short cannot afford the time to capture it.

Particularly when Kasparov is piling on the pressure with moves like ...

24 ♗f4!

... pin-pointing a fresh weakness.

24 ...	♛d7
25 h3	♜d8
26 ♕e4	

Emphasising White's control of the open file and looking towards the kingside. Black is actually running very short of decent moves. If, for instance, 26...♛c7,

then 27 ♕f5, creeping into Black's position, with the idea of 27...♛xa5 28 ♗xd6!.

| 26 ... | h5 |

This was criticised after the game, in my view unfairly, for it allows White to engineer a breakthrough on the kingside. True enough, but waiting was also not a terribly attractive proposition. Kasparov could have played 27 g4 and begun a slow and painful press on the kingside anyway.

By this point both players were running seriously short of time: both had just six minutes to play 14 moves, which accounts for Kasparov's next move—it has no real purpose, but as he has complete control of the position it certainly does no harm, and more to the point, he played it quickly.

27 ♜e2	g6
28 ♕f3!	♗g7
29 ♜e4	♗f8
30 ♕e2	

Kasparov still maintains control over the open file, but has cleverly swapped around the position of his queen and rook. This enables the queen to support the g4 break, and the threat of the rook penetrating down the e-file is more worrying for Black than the queen.

| 30 ... | ♛c7 |

The threat to the a-pawn forces Kasparov into activity.

| 31 ♗g5 | ♜c8 |

With hindsight this is not the best square for the rook; moving to a8 immediately would have been better.

32 g4!

While Short's queen and rook are redundant on the queenside, Kasparov cracks open the other wing. His domination of the e-file effectively cuts Short's position in two, preventing the heavy pieces from coming across to defend the king.

32 ... hxg4

33 ♗f6!?

This came as a great surprise. With just a couple of minutes left to reach move forty and Short down to his final minute, Kasparov gambles, giving up a pawn but gaining time in his lunge for the king.

The slow build-up of the earlier part of the game, almost reminiscent of Karpov, is left behind; this dynamic sacrifice of a pawn is pure Kasparov. Any other chessplayer would have simply recaptured the pawn here, 33 hxg4, retaining excellent attacking chances.

33 ... gxh3

34 ♕g4 ♖a8?

A mistake. Short should have blocked out the bishop immediately with 34...♗g7; in his terrible time pressure he must have missed that after 35 ♖e7, he could simply give up his queen, 35...♗xf6 36 ♖xc7 ♖xc7, to reach a position where White is unable to break through—it is a positional draw.

35 ♕xh3

The most natural move, but Kasparov claimed afterwards that 35 ♕g5 would have been decisive: 35...♗g7 36 ♖h4 ♕d7 37 ♗xg7 ♔xg7 38 ♕h6+ ♔f6 39 ♖f4+, and now if 39...♔e7 40 ♕h4+ and ♕h8+ wins a rook, or 39...♔e5 40 ♕g5+ f5 41 f3! and ♖e4 mate.

35 ... ♗g7

36 ♗xg7?

Kasparov persists with his attack, but later analysis confirmed that 36 ♖e7 was correct. Black must play 38...♕c8 (38...♕xa5 39 ♖xf7 ♔xf7 40 ♕e6+ wins) 39 ♕xc8+ ♖xc8 40 ♗xg7 ♔xg7 41 ♖d7 with excellent winning prospects for White.

36 ... ♔xg7

37 ♖h4

This looks decisive, but with just seconds left on his clock Short finds the only defence.

37 ... ♖g8!

This allows the king to slip safely to the queenside. It was quite clear from Kasparov's pained expression that he had overlooked this defence. He shook his

head, then glanced at the clock,
saw that he was down to his final
minute and bashed out his next
move ...

38   ♖h7+

... and as he did so, offered a
draw. Short hesitated for a moment before playing:

38 ...   ♚f8

He didn't bother to reply to
Kasparov's draw offer—he hardly
had time to. With a clear pawn
more, and his king running to
safety, the onus is on Kasparov to
prove that his attack is good
enough.

39   ♕g4

This is a 'pass' move, but the
most important thing was that it
was made instantly. Short reached
for his king, but hesitated for a
split second before playing:

39 ...   ♚e8

He played the move, but as he
pressed the button on top of the
clock, his flag fell. The arbiters,
Yuri Averbakh and Carlos Falcon,
stepped in and it was quickly established that Short had failed to
make the required forty moves.
After the players had signed the
scoresheets, Averbakh stepped to
the front of the stage and announced that **Short had lost on
time**.

Nigel put a brave face on it,
and even stayed to analyse a couple of critical moments with Kasparov.

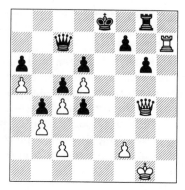

In the final position Kasparov
declared that he would have
played 40 ♕e6+, but this leads to
a winning endgame for Black:
40...fxe6 41 ♖xc7 exd5 42 cxd5
♖f8!, with the idea ...♖f3-c3 and
...♖xc2; or perhaps just ...♖f5 and
...♖xd5.

Instead of 40 ♕e6+, White
could wait with 40 ♚g2, but this
allows Black to slowly unravel
with 40...♖f8, ...♕d7, and ...♚e8-
d8-c7. Once the king reaches safety
on the queenside, Black can begin
to exploit his extra pawn.

A tragedy for Nigel. He was under great pressure but kept his
head, and when Kasparov made a
mistake in the execution of his attack, took his chance. Just a moment's hesitation at the end cost
him the game—though of course
Kasparov must take great credit
for keeping up the pressure on
Short's position.

The score: 1-0 in Kasparov's favour.

Game 2

Short-Kasparov
Sicilian Najdorf

By the next morning, however, Short's supporters were putting a better gloss on events. *The Times*, naturally eager to sustain the illusion of a close sp⌐rting contest, began to present the first game in a wholly different light. 'Early Victory Slips from Short's Grasp' was one headline, followed the next day by an even more optimistic note, 'Short Campaign Claims Moral Victory in Defeat by Clock'.

So, in the space of 48 hours, a disaster had been transformed into a 'moral victory'. Kasparov chose not to contest this view, doubtless content with his real one. 'Was it a moral victory?' asked Leonard Barden, the veteran chess writer who had marked out Kasparov as a future world champion at the age of 12. 'I feel the better poker player won.'

After overnight analysis there was a growing consensus among the grandmasters that Short might have had a winning position if only he had cleared the hurdle of the time control. It also emerged (which Kasparov had not revealed at the press conference after the game) that he had offered a draw in the time scramble, which Short had declined because he was one pawn ahead. It struck me that Short's mind must now be in turmoil. He might have had a win; he could certainly have had a draw; yet he had ended up with a humiliating defeat.

Some British players who knew Short well were admitting already to fears that he might think himself jinxed, as he had always seemed to be in the past when playing Kasparov. In their last 15 games he had drawn four and lost eleven. A friend said Short had consoled himself in his hotel by playing with his two-year-old daughter, Kiveli, and strumming his guitar. His wife, Rea, herself a psychotherapist, had doubtless also played her part in lifting what must have been a profoundly unsettled mood.

On the other hand, Short had a habit of losing the first game in all his big matches and coming back off the floor. Raymond Keene had written before the match: 'One of Short's strengths, perhaps his greatest, is his immense resilience.' He was clearly having to call on that resilience rather earlier in the contest than he had planned.

Kasparov pointed out, though, that every player feels the pressure of his first game in a world championship. In his own case, he had gone

5-0 down against Karpov in 1984 and did not score a win until the thirty-second game. Had his first challenge been restricted to the 24 games scheduled for this match, he would have lost, and the whole of modern chess history would have had to be rewritten.

As the second game was in progress, a colleague said to me in the press room: 'Have you noticed how the champion is behaving himself?' It was true. Kasparov had not risen to any of the pre-match insults hurled at him by his opponent. He had also been scrupulous in his conduct at the chessboard. Leonard Barden described him in the *Guardian* as 'a model of correctness. He shook hands briefly, avoiding the so-called KGB handshake he sometimes practises, in which he grasps his rival's hand until he can establish penetrating eye contact. He made no attempt to gaze at the Briton during play.'

At the table Kasparov would rub his nose or scratch his ear, but his most common pose was holding his head in his hands and staring through them tunnel-like in fierce concentration at the board, occasionally looking up abstractedly at the audience without really seeing them.

Short sits stiffly, a throbbing vein in his forehead, looking tense and stern, a schoolboy trying out the headmaster's chair. He looks round quite often at the display boards, as if in search of inspiration or to see his board position from a different perspective. He has a habit of holding his hands over his ears, as if to shut out insistent inner voices. As Keene put it, 'Chess is a game that invites paranoia, and not without justification.'

Meanwhile, there was paranoia behind the scenes when Channel 4, which had exclusive rights to film the live action, found that the BBC had set up shop in the theatre manager's office. Mike Miller, the channel's commissioning editor, said grimly: 'We expressed our displeasure to the Savoy. As far as we are concerned, the BBC are out of there – or there will be trouble.'

Short arrived in a black suit to play White in an aggressive opening to the second game. Although he put Kasparov under pressure, a complex, fluctuating game ended in an honourable draw, with grandmasters disagreeing afterwards as to which player had the advantage. Of the challenger's performance, his manager, Michael Stean, was heard to say: 'You ain't seen nothing yet.' Nobody felt disposed to argue with that.

1 e4

Short opens with his favourite first move.

1 ... c5

As does Kasparov. The Sicilian Defence is poorly named: 'Counter-attack' would be more accurate. Although initially White would seem to have the better attacking prospects, Black relies on his excellent pawn structure to hold the fort, while launching counterplay on the queenside.

2 ♘f3 d6
3 d4 cxd4
4 ♘xd4 ♘f6
5 ♘c3 a6

The Najdorf Variation, named after Miguel Najdorf, the Polish-Argentinian who was one of the strongest players in the world in the 1950s. Since then, its uncompromising stance (based on the sacrifice of development for better pawn structure) has attracted many strong players, most notably Bobby Fischer, who developed some of the key ideas.

6 ♗g5

Short shows that he is ready for a fight. This is the sharpest of all White's sixth move options.

6 ... ♘c6

As in game 1, Kasparov steers clear of the most critical continuation (6...e6), once again concerned that he could get caught in Short's home preparation. A pragmatic and sensible decision. A great deal has been written about Kasparov's daring openings, but more often than not they are the result of painstaking home analysis before a single move is played in an actual fight.

7 ♕d2 e6

The game has transposed into a 'Richter-Rauzer', named after Kurt Richter, a German master, and Vsevolod Rauzer, a Russian, who developed the system (independently) for White in the 1930s.

8 0-0-0 ♗d7
9 f4 h6
10 ♗h4 g5!?

Not as crazy as it looks. The idea is to break up White's dangerous central pawn front—and of course the move has been seen before.

11 fxg5 ♘g4

This is the trick: Short cannot move the pawn on g5 because of ...♕xh4.

12 ♘f3

Nigel selects a sensible continuation, returning the pawn immediately, but retaining long-term attacking prospects. It was possible to play a more critical continuation (from a theoretical point of view) but why risk walking into some of Kasparov's home analysis?

12 ...   hxg5
13 ♗g3

This is forced. Nigel thought for a few agonising moments before making his move, presumably just familiarising himself with the variation, though giving those of us watching a heart attack. If White takes the pawn, 13 ♗xg5, then Black wins material in surprising fashion: 13...f6 14 ♗f4 e5 15 ♗e3 ♘xe3 16 ♕xe3 ♗h6, and the queen is pinned against the king.

13 ...   ♗e7
14 ♗e2   ♘ge5

Both sides can be satisfied with their opening: Short has open lines for his pieces and therefore some attacking prospects against Black's king; whilst Kasparov has an excellent square for his knight on e5, a compact central pawn structure (an asset in the long term), and some counter-attacking chances down the open c-file. Chances are balanced.

15 ♔b1

Tucking the king in the corner before deciding on a middlegame plan.

15 ...   b5

Beginning operations on the queenside.

16 ♖df1

The rook comes to the open f-file, pointing in the direction of Black's king, and at the same time vacates the d1 square for the knight in case Kasparov should push the pawn to b4.

16 ...   ♖c8

Kasparov brings his rook to the open c-file in typical Sicilian fashion, but in so doing he burns his boats: the king can no longer escape to the queenside by castling if Short launches an attack in the middle.

17 ♘xe5

Short spent about a quarter of an hour on this move, and it was time well invested: he has come up with a plan which is straightforward and strong.

17 ...   ♘xe5
18 ♖f2

This is the idea: Short wants to double rooks on the f-file, increasing the pressure on Kasparov's king.

18 ...   f6
19 ♖hf1

Short remains consistent to his plan, but I'm sure he would have been tempted by 19 h4 attempting to open the kingside.

Although both players were moving reasonably quickly in the early part of the game, they slowed up over the past few moves as they delved into the complexities of the middlegame. It is clear that another time scramble is brewing. The clock times at this point: Short had used 1 hour 19 minutes; and Kasparov 1 hour 15 minutes. Before two hours is up they must both have made forty moves or they forfeit on time—as Short did in the first game.

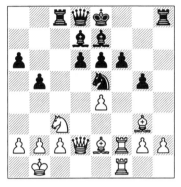

19 ... ♗c6
20 a3

Necessary, as Kasparov was threatening to play 20...b4 and ...♗xe4.

A natural plan for Black now would be to play 20...♖b8 with the idea of breaking open Short's king position with ...b4; but then White might well consider 21 ♕d1 threatening ♗h5+, e.g. 21...b4 22 axb4 ♖xb4 23 ♗h5+ ♔d7 (23...♔f8 24 ♗xe5 dxe5 25 ♖xf6+! ♗xf6 26 ♕xd8+) 24 ♗xe5 fxe5 25 ♗g4! with the threat of ♗xe6+ and ♕g4 mate, as well as ♘d5!. A good illustration of White's attacking prospects.

20 ... ♗b7
21 h3

Most onlookers were baffled by Short's choice of move here: he played it very quickly, though its purpose is uncertain. 21 ♕d1! with similar variations to the previous note, would have been more to the point. Kasparov was clearly worried about the attacking potential of Short's light-squared bishop and on the next move forced its exchange—even at the cost of giving up his beautifully centralised knight.

21 ... ♘c4!
22 ♗xc4

If instead 22 ♕d1, then 22...♘xa3+! wins a pawn.

22 ... ♖xc4
23 ♕d3

Short is toying with the idea of playing e5, followed by landing a big check on g6. Kasparov's next rules out this possibility.

23 ... e5

The position is still dynamically balanced: White's king is more secure than Black's (better pawn cover), but Black's central pawn mass and two bishops will be strong assets if the queens are exchanged. To add to the complications both players are running perilously short of time.

24 ♖e2 ♕c8
25 ♖f5?

An incomprehensible move—even to Short after the game. He sends the rook up a blind alley from which it can only return—thus costing him two moves.

In view of Kasparov's reply, 25 ♗e1 suggests itself instead. The bishop is biting on reinforced concrete on the g3 square, and will eventually find a more useful diagonal on the queenside.

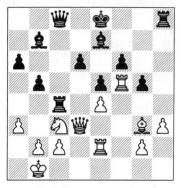

25 ...   Ξxc3

A classic Sicilian exchange sacrifice—Black removes one of White's most dangerous attacking pieces and at the same time shatters the queenside pawns. It is suddenly White's king, rather than Black's, which looks insecure.

But was such drastic action necessary? Immediately after the game when interviewed on Channel 4 television, Kasparov admitted that: 'There were perhaps better moves, but I think it was a good practical choice as I had little time left. After that my moves are very easy to play.'

Certainly Short looked surprised at Kasparov's decision, but admitted afterwards that he had 'underestimated the sacrifice'.

26 bxc3

Short chooses to keep the queens on—a decision which we

applauded in the television studio, as we felt that Black would have the initiative in the endgame playing against the doubled c-pawns. With the queens remaining Short still has chances to attack Kasparov's king if the position breaks open—though it's a gamble because his own king is insecure.

26 ...   ♕e6
27 ♔b2   ♔d7
28 Ξf1!

At least Short is able to admit his mistakes: the rook does nothing on f5.

28 ...   ♕c4?

Kasparov was quite damning about this move after the game—'a terrible mistake'—though given that he was approaching serious time pressure I think his desire to simplify the position is understandable. He mentioned instead 28...♗c6, with the idea ...a5, and possibly ...Ξb8 and ...b4 breaking open the queenside, with attacking chances.

White's problem is that it is very difficult to find any weakness in Black's position to aim at. 29 Ξh1 with the idea of 30 h4 suggests itself, if only to keep Black's rook busy. I cannot believe that White stands worse here, though in so saying I'm contradicting the mighty Gazza himself.

29 ♕xc4

Short leapt at the chance to exchange queens here: in distinction to the previous position, his weak c-pawns are masked by a black pawn.

29	...	bxc4
30	♔a2	♝c6
31	♖b1!	♝d8
32	♖b8!	

It is essential to get some active play before Kasparov is allowed to advance his central pawn mass—their time has almost come. For the first time in the match we began to feel truly optimistic about Short's chances: Kasparov had less than five minutes to make his remaining nine moves—and the position looked to be turning against him.

| 32 | ... | ♖e8! |

Kasparov finds the only correct way to expel the rook; there were certainly plenty of chances to go wrong, e.g. 32...♔c7? 33 ♖b4 d5 34 exd5 ♝xd5 35 ♖xe5!.

| 33 | ♝f2 | ♝a5 |

The exchange of rooks is favourable to White in positions of this kind (rooks generally work very well with bishops), but Kasparov had to go in for it: Short was threatening to exchange bishops with 34 ♝b6. Black's bishop pair is his most important asset.

34	♖xe8	♔xe8
35	♔b2	♔f7
36	♝a7	

A bizarre-looking move, but the bishop clears out of the way of the rook, and it is useful to have the option of moving to b8.

Kasparov was now into his final minute and Short had only a little more.

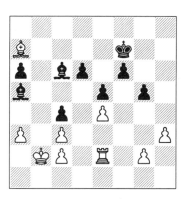

| 36 | ... | ♔e6 |
| 37 | g4? | |

I must admit that I applauded this move when it was played—the pessimist in me could only picture Black's centre pawns screaming down the board, hassling the rook, the white king trapped in the corner unable to prevent their advance. A nightmare scenario.

It's true that the advance of the g-pawn prevents Black breaking with ...f5, but it reduces White's own winning chances. Upon reflection 37 g3!, with the idea of 38 h4, creating an outside passed pawn, is more dangerous for Black than White, for example: 37...f5 38 exf5+ ♔xf5 39 ♝b8! ♔e6 40 ♖d2! ♝d5 41 h4. Black's centre pawns are stymied, while the h-pawn is an express.

37	...	♝d8
38	♔c1	♝e7
39	♖e3	d5

40 exd5+   ♔xd5

The time control has been made—with just seconds to spare. Short played his 41st move after little reflection ...

41 ♔b2

... and exited the stage to cool off for a few moments. Looking at the monitor in his rest room, he must have realised that the moment had passed for him, and indeed that he would have to play carefully in order to hold the draw. The problem is that his king is tied to the defence of the a-pawn; the h3 pawn is weak; Black's e-pawn is dangerous; the bishop pair is potent. More than adequate compensation for the exchange.

41 ..   ♔e6
42 ♗b6   ♗d6
43 h4!

Short cuts his losses and takes steps to simplify the position.

43 ...   gxh4
44 ♖h3   e4
45 ♖xh4   ♗f4

46 ♖h3   ♗g5
47 ♗d4   a5
48 ♖h2   a4
49 ♖h1   ♗d7
50 ♖h2   ♔d5

If Short passively defends the g-pawn with 51 ♖g2, then he risks losing after 51...e3 and 52...♔e4; instead he wisely forces simplification into a drawn ending.

51 ♖h5

Instead of dragging the game out with 51...♗xg4 52 ♖xg5+ fxg5 53 ♗e3 ♔e5 54 ♗xg5 reaching a barren ending, Kasparov shrugged his shoulders and offered a draw which Short accepted immediately.

Interviewed after the game, both players seemed reasonably satisfied. Kasparov was visibly relieved that he had held the game and generously praised the challenger's play; and Short can take heart from the fact that he had worried the champion and came close to winning.

The score: 1½-½ to Kasparov.

Game 3

Kasparov-Short
Ruy Lopez, Anti-Marshall

Short, by this time, had become openly contemptuous of his critics – or, as he revealingly called them, 'my *enemies*'. In the *Daily Telegraph* I had quoted some British grandmasters who feared that Short might be 'whitewashed', by which they meant he might not win a game. This infuriated him. 'Most of these people don't know what they're talking about,' he declared. These signs of a 'bunker mentality' were not encouraging, especially so soon into the match. One began to fear for him.

This fear was not, apparently, shared by his two-year-old daughter, Kiveli, who was heard to say loudly after move 20 in the Grandmasters' room: 'Daddy is winning!' Alas, she was to prove mistaken and Kasparov won his second game out of three, though the champion admitted afterwards to 'a little luck'. Short responded sharply: 'You make your own luck.' He was unconsciously echoing the Cuban genius, Capablanca, who once said: 'The good chess player is always lucky.'

Novelist Julian Barnes, who was covering the event for the *New Yorker*, was reflecting quietly in the Grandmasters' room on the role that luck played in chess. Like Short and Capablanca, he didn't really believe in it. His general thesis, as I recall, went like this: 'When a player makes the right move, even without understanding all its implications, it still isn't luck if it succeeds. At this level there are all sorts of hidden, half-conscious, half-remembered factors in making a move that have nothing to do with luck and everything to do with instinct and experience. They are a part of what we mean when we talk about a talent for the game.'

Kasparov introduced another abstract concept, truth, in an interview immediately after the third game: 'I always felt that the *truth* was on my side.' What he meant was probably not metaphysical at all, but that the innate chess logic of the position was in his favour. He clearly thought that Short's attack in the third game had been too risky, not supported by the objective reality – or 'truth' – of his position.

A foreign chess writer of philosophical bent took me aside in the press room, not for the first time, and said of Short's attacking gambit in the third game: 'Nigel might have got away with that against most players, because they might well have made a mistake under the pressure

Short created, but not Kasparov. You can't base your game against Kasparov on the hope that he will make a mistake. Karpov would never have done that.'

Simon Barnes, a subtle sports writer for *The Times*, drew analogies with other games, wondering if Short was already playing like a man who knew his only chance of a comeback was to throw caution to the winds, like Ian Botham at Headingley in 1981. 'The question that we and Short must address is whether this was a strong, confident and bold piece of counter-attacking play that didn't quite come off – or whether this was the hopeless slog of an already defeated man.'

Short's loyal friend, Dominic Lawson, said 'the attack blew like a hurricane through the champion's apparently invulnerable kingside defences. I am not indulging in hyperbole when I say that the audience in the Savoy Theatre was gasping in disbelief at the audacity of Short's sacrificial attack.'

Reading that aloud from the *Daily Telegraph* to the press room at large, a more sceptical soul raised a laugh when he remarked: 'Yeah, OK. But he still bloody lost, didn't he?'

1	e4	e5
2	♘f3	♘c6
3	♗b5	a6
4	♗a4	♘f6
5	0-0	♗e7
6	♖e1	b5
7	♗b3	0-0

So far, everything as game 1. The question is: will Kasparov take on Short's Marshall Gambit?

8 a4

No. Against all predictions, Kasparov repeats his quiet opening from the first game. The champion has a reputation for playing the most critical lines in the opening, so his approach here goes against the grain.

8 ...   ♗b7

Short is the first one to deviate from game 1. This is the most common method of replying to 8 a4, and has a better reputation than the perhaps over-committal 8...b4.

9 d3   ♖e8

9...d6 is a more usual continuation. By delaying the d-pawn's advance, Short is perhaps hoping to play ...d5 in one move.

10 ♘bd2

The theoretically recommended move for White in this position is 10 ♘c3, but Kasparov continues his cautious approach from game 1, preferring to build the tension rather than lock antlers at an early stage.

10 ...   ♗f8

A common manoeuvre. The bishop drops back one square allowing the rook more influence over the centre.

11 c3   h6

A safe move, preventing a possible ♘g5 attacking f7 (although at the moment this point can be defended by ...♖e7). However, with hindsight, 11...h6 creates a slight weakness which Kasparov pounces on in a couple of moves.

Note that 11...d5 fails to 12 exd5 ♘xd5 13 d4 (13...exd4? 14 ♖xe8 ♕xe8 15 ♗xd5).

12 ♗a2!

This subtle move is terribly strong. The bishop moves out of range of the knight on c6, and leaves Black searching for a meaningful plan.

12 ...   d6

Kasparov has two promising continuations after this. 12...b4 would have been better.

13 ♘h4!

The bishop on a2 makes its presence felt. Kasparov is not launching a violent attack, but rather making a hit and run raid to exchange off knight for bishop.

There is no doubting the strength of Kasparov's move, but

did he have something better? Debate in the press room was centred on the possibility of 13 axb5 axb5 14 ♕b3! threatening the pawns on b5 and f7. The variations are extremely complicated, but so far no one has been able to find a satisfactory defence for Black, for example: 14...♕d7 15 ♕xb5 ♗a6 16 ♗xf7+! and 17 ♖xa6; or 15...♖a5 16 ♕xb7 ♖b8 17 ♕xb8 ♘xb8 18 ♗xf7+ and 19 ♖xa5, with a material advantage.

Both players refused to comment on this possibility after the game, just to add to the mystery.

13 ...   ♕d7

Attempting to stop the knight's invasion lands Black in even worse trouble: 13...♘e7 14 ♕f3!, with the idea of 15 ♘f1 threatening ♗xh6, leaves Black in a terrible mess.

14 ♘g6

It is still possible to speculate on an attack with 14 ♕f3, or perhaps 14 h3 preventing a queen exchange, but years of playing against Karpov have taught the champion to prefer a long-term advantage to a short-term initiative.

14 ...   ♘e7
15 ♘xf8   ♔xf8

Most of us watching the game felt that, in spite of Kasparov's possession of the bishop pair, Short's position was solid enough, and he should have reasonable defensive chances. The champion's next move disabused us of such

comforting thoughts. He thought
for fifteen minutes before playing:

16 f3!

For me, this subtle pawn advance is the strongest move of the
game. As Short himself said the
following day in *The Times*: 'This
is an excellent move. It bolsters
up Kasparov's centre and places
a granite block in the path of my
queen's bishop. I did not see this
coming but now I recall that Kasparov did something similar in a
brilliant game [Game 1] against
Karpov in their last championship match at New York in 1990.'

White has several plans to
choose from in the position—perhaps breaking with d4, perhaps
moving the knight to f1 or b3—
and it is terribly important to
keep options open. 16 f3 not only
bolsters the e4 pawn, but it is also
a high-class waiting move, waiting to see where Short puts his
pieces before deciding on a plan.

16 ...	Iad8
17 b4!	♘g6
18 ♘b3	♗c8
19 ♗b1	♘h5!

Kasparov's bishops look pas-
sive on the back rank, but whenever the position breaks open
they will rule the board; and
thanks to the excellent knight
manoeuvre ♘d2-b3, he has gained
control of the queenside. Short
makes an accurate assessment of
the position and realises that his
only chance lies in a direct attack
on the king.

20 axb5	axb5
21 ♗e3	♘h4
22 Ia2!	

An excellent defensive move.
The rook maintains control over
the open a-file as well as defending the king—and another point
to the move 16 f3 is revealed.

22 ...	Ie6

Blunt and risky—but the only
chance. If Short doesn't break
through, the rook will be stranded
offside, disconnected from the
rest of its forces.

23 d4	Ig6
24 ♔h1	

If instead 24 dxe5? ♕h3! is the
end for White.

24 ...	Ie8
25 dxe5	Ixe5!

The only try. Allowing an exchange of queens would be hopeless because of the weakened
queenside, and actually loses
material straightaway: 25...dxe5
26 ♕xd7 ♗xd7 27 ♗f2! ♘xg2 28
♗c5+ and 29 Ixg2.

26 g4!

Played on intuition more than

anything else. It's not just that Black's knight is attacked, the pawn blocks out the rook and queen from the attack—for the time being at least.

26 ...   Rf6

Moving the knight back to f6 would mean the end of the attack, so Short is forced to improvise.

27 &Bd4?

Kasparov must have only calculated 27...&Nxf3 28 &Bxe5 &Qxg4 29 &Rg1! with an overwhelming material advantage. He had obviously totally overlooked Short's spectacular reply.

27 &Nd4, defending f3, would have been a simple way to thwart the attack, for example, 27...&Nf4 28 &Nf5! and Black is in a mess.

27 ...   &Ng3+!

Kasparov looked shocked at this move, but with just a minute left, still keeps himself together.

28 hxg3   &Nxf3
29 &Bxe5   &Qxg4

Threatening ...&Qh3+; Kasparov's next move is forced.

30 &Rh2   &Nxe1!
31 &Qxe1

If 31 &Qxg4 &Rf1 mate.

31 ...   dxe5?

With no time left on his clock, Short makes the obvious recapture, but it's a mistake.

If he had flicked in 31...&Qf3+! first, with so little time, Kasparov would have been hard pressed to defend. After 32 &Kg1 dxe5, it would not be possible to bring the knight over to defend the king (as happened in the game): 33 &Nd2 &Qxc3! and with three pawns for the piece Black is surely in great shape.

Of course, White has better than 33 &Nd2, and indeed with precise play might still escape with his extra piece: 33 &Rd2! &Bh3! (preventing &Rd3) 34 &Nc5! &Rg6 35 &Kh2! &Qh5 35 &Bc2! and amazingly, Black has no good discovered check at his disposal, as Malcolm Pein pointed out in the *Daily Telegraph*. But would Kasparov have found such a string of exact moves with only a few remaining seconds on the clock?

32 ♘d2

After this excellent defensive move, the game is effectively over. Short can make no further progress with his attack and his pieces are driven back in disarray.

32	...	♖d6
33	♗c2	♗e6
34	♔g1	♔g8
35	♘f1	♕g5
36	♕e3	♕d8
37	♖d2	c6
38	♖xd6	♕xd6
39	♕c5	♕xc5+
40	bxc5	h5

The time scramble is over, and the smoke has cleared to reveal an endgame in which Short has just two pawns for a piece. Kasparov claimed afterwards that it would have been very difficult to win with correct play from Black. Maybe; but there must have been the thought in the back of Short's mind that if the game were to be adjourned, half of Moscow would

have been engaged to find a win. He didn't put much effort into the remaining moves.

41	♘d2	♔f8
42	♔f2	♔e7
43	♗b3	♗d7
44	♘f3	♔f6
45	c4	bxc4
46	♗xc4	♗e6
47	♗e2	♗g4
48	♗d1!	g6
49	♗a4!	♗d7
50	♘e1!	♔e6
51	♗b3+	♔e7
52	♘d3	f6
53	♘b4	f5
54	♗a4	fxe4
55	♗xc6	♗xc6
56	♘xc6+	♔e6
57	♔e3	g5

Or 57...♔d5 58 ♘e7+ and ♘xg6.

58	♔xe4	h4
59	gxh4	

And **Black resigned**.

A disappointment for Short who missed a good chance in time pressure. Kasparov was magnanimous in victory: 'The score is two and a half to a half in my favour, but it could easily have been the other way round.'

Perhaps he was a little too generous. Overall this was an excellent performance from Kasparov. He outplayed Short from the opening and played a superb middlegame; in time pressure he made one mistake which might have jeopardised the win, but thereafter he held his nerve.

Game 4

Short-Kasparov
Sicilian Najdorf

This was the game of 'the poisoned pawn'. As soon as this variation of the Sicilian Defence was deployed, the mighty minds at the Grandmasters' table went back to the Fischer-Spassky match in 1972, when the Russian had used it to achieve one of his rare sweeping victories. Among Fischer's seconds on that occasion was Lubomir Kavalek, now coaching Short. Had 'Lubosh' remembered this gambit and brought it out and polished it for Nigel after 21 years?

Whole books have been devoted to the theory and practice of 'the poisoned pawn', so the grandmasters were in their element in the basement bar at Simpson's-in-the-Strand, moving pieces swiftly around their boards and shouting suggestions to each other as they tried to work out where the many options might lead.

It was a reminder of the infinite variety of a game of chess. After two moves by each side the number of possible positions on the board is 71,852. After three moves it is nine million. If you wanted to work out each possible variation after four moves, taking a minute for each one, it has been calculated that the process would last 600,000 years. The grandmasters moved rather faster than that.

So did Kasparov, who won a resounding victory just after the two-hour time control, giving him three wins out of the four games played. What surprised many observers was that this had not been achieved by the champion's own daring and imaginative play, as people had come to expect, but by cautious counterplay in response to aggressive attacks by Short. What was going on here?

The players' own opinions on their performance and the state of the match emerged in various ways. The winner (both players if it was a draw) appeared at a press conference after the game to answer journalists' questions on the Savoy Theatre stage. They gave interviews to Channel 4. They spoke privately to Ray Keene and other staff of *The Times*, who used the information to flesh out their extensive game analysis.

But, in the way of the chess world, stories also seeped out through officials and friends and friends of friends, and little stayed secret for long, despite the diligent efforts of the franchise-holders to retain their expensively acquired exclusivity. One journalist who happened to shake hands with Short soon after his ill-fated fourth game, for example, said: 'It was like being given a handful of spaghetti.' There was no need for an exclusive quote to know that the challenger was in bad shape. The body language said it all.

So, with the score at 3.5 to 0.5, we knew who to blame: as ever, it was all the fault of the media, who had apparently been pressuring Short to play too sharply. By now the bookmakers were refusing to take any more bets on Kasparov winning the match. Odds on Short were 12-1 and you could get 3-1 on him not winning a single game. No wonder one of his friends described him as being 'in a trough of depression'.

After such a shattering start, how will Short play? Will he put a brake on today, or will he continue his aggressive policy? There were many who counselled caution, but Nigel was to remain true to himself and willingly entered into a bloody battle.

1	e4	c5
2	♘f3	d6
3	d4	cxd4
4	♘xd4	♘f6
5	♘c3	a6

The Najdorf Variation once again: Kasparov is eager to take up the fight.

6 ♗g5

And Nigel repeats this aggressive bishop move from game 2. This time, instead of backing off from a theoretical fight, Kasparov courts one—after four days' preparation:

| 6 | ... | e6 |
| 7 | f4 | ♕b6 |

The notorious 'Poisoned Pawn' Variation, a favourite of Kasparov's and before him Fischer. Whole books have been written about its wild complications—without coming to any definite conclusion. In outrageous fashion, Black's queen makes an early sortie for just a measly pawn, leaving the rest of his pieces on the back rank, and his king exposed to a violent attack from White's mobilised forces. Remarkably, Black seems to get away with it—for most of the time at any rate.

It is possible to defend the pawn, 8 ♘b3 is the best way, but this takes away a dangerous attacking piece from the centre and is not a serious test of the opening. But Short is ready for a fight, and freely sacrifices the pawn.

| 8 | ♕d2 | ♕xb2 |
| 9 | ♘b3 | |

9 ♖b1 is more usual, but Short obviously has something evil prepared.

| 9 | ... | ♕a3 |
| 10 | ♗xf6 | gxf6 |

By doubling the pawns, White ensures that Black's king will remain in the centre for some time: the kingside is too full of holes.

11	♗e2	♘c6
12	0-0	♗d7
13	♔h1	h5

Ruling out the possibility of White playing the bishop into h5.

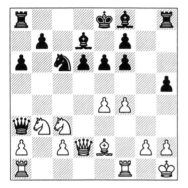

This position has been seen several times before, most notably in the 11th game of the 1972 world championship match in which Spassky played 14 ♘b1!? here, routing Fischer in just 31 moves. Improvements were later found for Black in this particular line, but the mysteries of the whole position have not yet been fully explored. Short's next move has been played once before, in an obscure Soviet game from 1963, though from this moment the game is really off the beaten track. One of Nigel's seconds, Lubosh Kavalek, had worked with Fischer in Reykjavik in 1972, and there was speculation that this was the fruit of their labours—and that the idea was only being seen after 21 years.

14 ♘d1

Kasparov plunged into thought after Short's new or, perhaps I should say, resurrected idea. The knight move looks bizarre at first sight, but if it can hop round to c4 (via e3) then there are chances to attack Black's queen, and at the same time it eyes the b6 and d6 squares.

14	...		♖c8
15	♘e3		♕b4
16	c3		

Short was still playing his moves quite quickly as though all this was part of his opening preparation. Kasparov has a choice between grabbing another pawn and braving the attack, or playing more cautiously by retreating the queen immediately.

16 ... ♕xe4

We were amazed by this capture in the TV commentary room. After 16...♕b6 17 ♘c4 ♕c7 18 ♖fd1 White may regain the pawn on d6, but following all the exchanges on d6, it is a moot point as to how much advantage White has, if any.

At this point the clock times were, Short: 22 minutes, Kasparov: 1 hour 11 minutes. With Short moving quickly and confidently, there were many players predicting that Kasparov's blood would be spilt: Nigel must have it all worked out.

17 ♗d3

Also played quickly by Short. After the game, Kasparov declared that he was actually more afraid of 17 ♘c4, though 17...♘d8 creates a square for the queen to drop back to on c6.

    17 ...   **♛a4**
    18 ♘c4   **♜c7**

Nigel thought over his next move for 24 minutes, during which time we were wondering as to exactly where his home preparation had finished. 18...♜c7 cannot have been a surprise, and yet up to this moment he had been playing his moves quickly.

Here, we could see nothing better for Short than to take a draw by permanently attacking Kasparov's queen with the knight—though this would hardly have been a triumph for his homework.

What had gone wrong? Kasparov later said that objectively, Short should take the draw.

    19 ♘b6   **♛a3**

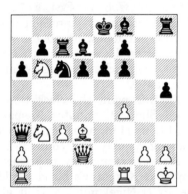

Now if Short wants a draw, he can simply play the knight back to c4 attacking the queen; and this was where the stubborn side of Short's character displayed itself.

He doesn't like to admit that he has made a mistake, and instead of swallowing his pride and taking the draw—which at such an early stage in the match would not have been greatly significant—he continued the struggle.

He admitted in *The Times* the next day: 'I have over-reacted by trying to annihilate him and been caught on the rebound. Perhaps there has been too much media pressure of the "Go on Nige, go in and get him" type. It would have been more prudent to keep my head down. But it is not in my character to wimp out of sharp positions.'

    20 ♖ae1   **♘e7!**
    21 ♘c4   **♖xc4**
    22 ♗xc4

Kasparov has given up rook for knight but has two extra pawns, a rough material balance, but from this moment Short's position deteriorates.

    22 ...   **h4**
    23 ♗d3

Short was worried about the knight coming into f5, with a possible sacrifice on g3, but this is not as dangerous as it appears. Playing the bishop back to e2 immediately would have saved time.

    23 ...   **f5**
    24 ♗e2   **♗g7**
    25 c4   **h3!**

Now White's king is permanently exposed.

    26 g3   **d5**
    27 ♗f3?

The decisive mistake. 27 cxd5 ♘xd5 28 ♗f3 keeps White in the game, though after 28...0-0 Kasparov has the better position due to his powerful bishops. Short's move is based on a miscalculation.

27 ... **dxc4**

Short thought that he could now play 28 ♖d1, and after 28...♘d5 29 ♗xd5 exd5, deliver checkmate with 30 ♕xd5 ♗c6 31 ♖fe1+ ♔f8 32 ♕xc6 bxc6 33 ♖d8 mate. Sweet dreams. Instead of 31...♔f8, Black can play either 31...♕e7, or 31...♗e5, which both win.

Nigel looked devastated. He finds a way to continue the struggle, but really his position from here on is hopeless.

28 ♖e3

A shallow trap. If 28...cxb3 29 ♖xb3 ♕c5 30 ♖xb7 with counterplay, but Kasparov took just a minute to play instead:

28 ... **c3**
29 ♖xc3

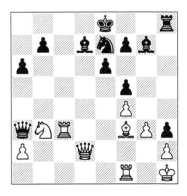

The passed pawn was too strong to be left, but now Short is two pawns down for nothing.

29 ... **♗xc3**
30 ♕xc3 **0-0**
31 ♖g1 **♖c8**
32 ♕f6 **♗c6**
33 ♗xc6 **♖xc6**
34 g4

It is easy to defend against this attack. In reality it is White's king that is the more exposed.

34 ... **♘g6**
35 gxf5 **exf5**
36 ♕xf5 **♕xa2**
37 ♕xh3 **♕c2**
38 f5 **♖c3**
39 ♕g4

In time pressure, Short misses his last chance, 39 ♘d4, but the ending after 39...♕e4+ 40 ♕g2 ♕xg2+ 41 ♔xg2 ♘e5 should be winning with care.

39 ... **♖xb3**
40 fxg6 **♕c6+**

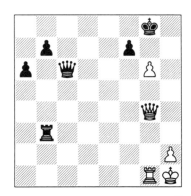

Here **White resigned**. If 41 ♖g2 ♖b1+; or 41 ♕g2 ♕xg2+ 42 ♔xg2 fxg6.

A curious and disappointing game from Short: where exactly did his preparation end, and which move of Kasparov's did he miss?

Having had his opening innovation defused, he then failed to re-adjust to having no real initiative and played too boldly, eventually making an appalling blunder.

When interviewed by Channel 4 TV after the game, Kasparov made the prescient comment that Short had been listening to 'too much bad advice ... A world championship match is totally different from anything Nigel has experienced before. He should have been cautious at the beginning, not super-aggressive.'

The score: 3½-½ in Kasparov's favour.

Game 5

Kasparov-Short

Nimzo-Indian Defence

'Is Nigel Short afraid of Kasparov?' Even *The Times*, which had so far given the challenger the benefit of every doubt, felt obliged to ask the question. Its own answer, predictably, was: 'Not at all.' It is interesting, though, to read Martin Amis's essay on the Kasparov-Karpov battle of 1986, which happened to be republished in a book of his essays during the London championship.

Short is quoted as saying: 'When I played Karpov, it took me half an hour to get over my awe at playing the world champion. Then it was business as usual, just another game. With Kasparov – it's hard to describe. I found his presence uniquely disturbing. I have never faced such an intense player, never felt such energy and concentration, such will and desire burning across the board at me.'

Now, however, some years later, he is quoted as saying: 'I'm not afraid of him any more.' Nobody bothers to ask, of course, if Kasparov is afraid of Nigel Short. What mattered to the challenger in the fifth game was simply stopping the rot. This he achieved convincingly with an agreed draw after only 18 moves in a game that Short appeared to have prepared well with Speelman's help. The tall, bespectacled, long-haired Speelman appeared in the Grandmasters' room with a knowing smile during the game. Short described it as 'an aggressive draw, a controlled explosion.'

He was clearly more at ease with himself. According to Simon Barnes, his body language was in sharp contrast to his demeanour after the previous game. 'Short was like a victor,' he wrote. 'He *was* a victor: he had conquered himself. He threw his arms and legs about the place, made a series of weird, expansive gestures. For he had turned back the tide of defeat, not to mention defeatism.'

An unusual feature of the game was the comparative amount of time the players took to play it. Kasparov spent an hour and a half to Short's 11 minutes, one of the biggest differences in a world championship game that anyone could remember. The champion, who spent most of the time on-stage wiping his brow and holding his head in his hands, joked afterwards: 'I have now played five games while Nigel has played four.'

In the subsequent chat at Simpson's someone recalled that the Soviet grandmaster, David Bronstein, who drew with the great Botvinnik in a world championship duel he should have won in 1951, once took half an hour to make his first move. Victor Korchnoi once took an hour and a half over a single move. The longest thinking time ever recorded is two hours and twenty minutes by the Brazilian IM Trois.

Short's performance, carefully prepared and skilfully executed, was impressive after his run of defeats, suggesting that he had finally overcome his early stage-fright and emerged from his 'trough of depression'. His supporters were relieved that he was no longer, as Keene put it, 'trying to obliterate the champion with his bare hands'. Word got about among the professionals that Short had worked this game out without Kavalek's assistance. Nobody knew precisely what this foretold.

1 d4

Having essayed 1 e4 in his first two White games, Kasparov decides to broaden the front. Now Short will have something more to think about when preparing to play Black.

1	...	♘f6
2	c4	e6
3	♘c3	♗b4

Short accepts the invitation to play the Nimzo-Indian Defence, an opening system developed by Aron Nimzowitsch, one of the strongest players in the world during the 1920s, and also one of the game's most profound thinkers. If Short had wanted to steady the ship after a couple of losses, one might have expected him to play a solid Queen's Gambit (3...d5) rather than this potentially double-edged opening.

4 ♕c2

The move of the moment. Kasparov's revival of 4 ♕c2 – formerly

regarded as a tame continuation – has led to a renaissance in 1 d4.

4	...	d5
5	cxd5	exd5
6	♗g5	h6
7	♗h4	

If Kasparov had wanted to play it safe, then he could have exchanged on f6, but this is hardly a test for Black. In view of the score, he prefers to maintain the tension in the position to keep the pressure on Short.

7	...	c5
8	dxc5	

This variation has many famous precedents. One of the first games with it was between Keres, with the white pieces, and Botvinnik, Kasparov's early mentor, from the Absolute Soviet Championship of 1941. Keres played 8 0-0-0, but after 8...♗xc3 9 ♕xc3 g5 10 ♗g3 cxd4 11 ♕xd4 ♘c6 12 ♕a4 ♗f5 13 e3 ♖c8, his king was cut to ribbons.

This game is typical of the variation: Black has a strong initiative which puts White under great pressure; but if White is able to survive, then he has good chances to counter-attack due to Black's ragged pawn structure (the weak d-pawn and the pawn on g5).

8 ...   g5

Black has to break the pin on the knight if he is to launch an attack, but, as mentioned in the previous note, this is a risky move: Black must maintain his initiative or he will regret this rash advance.

9 ♗g3   ♘e4
10 e3

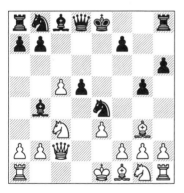

Instead of this, White could have taken on b8, initiating tremendous complications. A sample line: 10 ♗xb8 ♕f6! (10...♖xb8 11 ♕a4+ and ♕xb4) 11 ♕a4+ ♗d7 12 ♕xb4 ♕xf2+ 13 ♔d1 ♕xf1+ 14 ♔c2 ♕xa1.

10 ...   ♕a5

This logical continuation is the first new move of the game. Black reinforces the pressure on the pinned knight on c3, forcing White to defend when he would really rather be developing his kingside pieces. 10...♕f6 had been previously played in Goldin–Lautier, Palma de Mallorca 1989, but that allowed White to solve the problem of his development by playing 11 ♗b5+ ♗d7 12 ♗xd7+ ♘xd7 13 ♘ge2.

11 ♗e5

Kasparov thought for 25 minutes over this sensible move, defending the knight on c3 and at the same time attacking Black's rook on h8.

11 ...   0-0
12 ♗d3   ♘c6

12...♘xc3 13 ♗h7 mate, would not have been too bright. Nigel, however, has it all under control: he was still moving instantly while Kasparov's clock had pushed past the hour mark.

13 ♗xe4   ♘xe5
14 ♗xd5

It seemed to those of us watching that Kasparov had thought his way through Short's opening preparation, but Nigel's next move convinced us that all was still well:

14 ...   ♗g4!

Black prevents White from bringing his king to safety on the queenside. If now 15 f3, then 15...♕xc5! threatening e3 and d5.

15 ♘f3   ♗xf3
16 ♗xf3

Kasparov thought for almost twenty minutes before resigning himself to this prudent, but lifeless, capture. He realised that he would find himself in dire trouble if he tried to keep winning chances alive with 16 gxf3, e.g. 16...♖ac8 17 0-0 ♖xc5 18 ♗xb7 ♗xc3 19 bxc3 ♕c7! 20 ♗e4 f5! and Black crashes through on f3.

16	...	♘xf3+
17	gxf3	♖ac8
18	0-0	

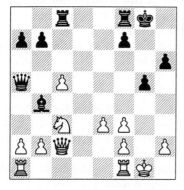

With this move Kasparov offered a **draw**, which Short accepted at once. After 18...♖xc5,

Black will then regain his second sacrificed pawn, if necessary by doubling rooks on the c-file, and the game fizzles out to a draw.

At the end of the game the clock times showed that Kasparov had used 1 hour 30 minutes, and Short just 11 minutes – the time that it had taken for him to walk back on stage before making each of his moves. It was obvious for all to see, Kasparov included, that the whole game was home preparation. As Short said afterwards: 'The final position was not unfamiliar to me.'

In their post-match TV interview Nigel looked distinctly chuffed, while Kasparov fidgeted uncomfortably, clearly embarrassed that one of his main opening weapons had been neutralised with such ease. There was already a look of revenge in his eye: 'I have some homework to do,' snarled the world champion ominously.

The score: 4-1 in Kasparov's favour.

Game 6

Short-Kasparov
Sicilian Najdorf

Could Short keep it up? In the sixth game he launched what Speelman called 'a vicious attack' and Keene 'a violent onslaught', sustaining his recovery and forcing the champion into a position from which he was visibly relieved to manage a draw. Generous applause greeted the end of what Nathan Divinsky, the Canadian chess expert, described as 'the most exciting day of the championship'.

Even so, the nagging doubt remained in the Grandmasters' room that Nigel had missed a good chance of a win, that he had forced the champion onto the ropes but settled for a draw instead of delivering the expected knock-out. At move 26 there was a loud groan among the grandmasters as the challenger failed to press home his advantage after Kasparov had made a palpable error a few moves before. International Master Andrew Martin was blunt: 'Short would have played the winning move against anyone else in the world. He's psyched out.'

The headline writers reflected this widely held view: 'Kasparov is Let off the Hook' (*Daily Telegraph*); 'Short Misses Another Chance' (*Guardian*); 'Short has Kasparov on Ropes but Fails to Deliver K.O. Punch' (*Sunday Times*). But was it a failure of nerve, or great defensive play by the champion? The grandmasters agreed in their daily bulletin : 'It is a tribute to Kasparov that even where calculation failed him, his intuition proved a sturdy second line of defence.' The champion himself admitted that he had 'panicked' at one point in the game and insisted: 'Short is back on track.'

Dominic Lawson argued that confidence was not the challenger's problem. 'If anything,' Lawson claimed, 'Short's approach to this match proves he is *over*-confident.' He attacked the press for suggesting otherwise: 'Too many of them seem to imagine chess is somehow a simple game, and that it is only neurosis which prevents a player like Short – or Kasparov for that matter – from playing the perfect move at every turn. Chess is a much more difficult, and much more interesting, game than that.'

Nonetheless, there was a growing feeling that the apparent inevitability of a Kasparov victory must be turning off the media. Eric Schiller, in charge of the press room, denied this, however, saying that over 350 journalists were still accredited to the match and that it 'may go down as one of the most interesting ever, no matter what the score is at the end.'

1	e4	c5
2	♘f3	d6
3	d4	cxd4
4	♘xd4	♘f6
5	♘c3	a6
6	♗c4	

So 6 ♗g5 has gone back into the garage for some repair work, and Short wheels out his next weapon against the Najdorf. The 6 ♗c4 variation was honed into a fearsome attacking system by Bobby Fischer in the 1960s, though antidotes to it were later found (notably by Fischer himself, playing the Black side!). In the past few years the system has enjoyed a revival – indeed Kasparov recently won a beautiful game on the White side against Gelfand in Linares.

6	...	e6

A sensible move, blocking the bishop's diagonal.

7	♗b3	♘bd7

The latest word in fashion. Until about five years ago everyone automatically played 7...b5 here instead.

8	f4	♘c5

The knight stands well on this square. It attacks the e4 pawn, bolsters the e6 square, and can chop off White's threatening bishop if it looks too dangerous.

9	f5	♗e7
10	♕f3	0-0

11 ♗e3

Normally, White would have castled by now (on the kingside), but this move indicates that Short is toying with the aggressive idea of putting his king on the queenside.

11 ...   e5

If Black doesn't take action in the centre he is likely to be overrun on the kingside. For instance, the game Winants-Christiansen, Holland 1993: 11...♗d7 12 g4! ♕a5 13 0-0-0 e5 14 ♘de2 ♘xb3+ 15 cxb3 ♗c6 16 ♘g3 ♖fd8 17 g5, and White won in just a few more moves with a direct attack on Black's king.

12 ♘de2   b5

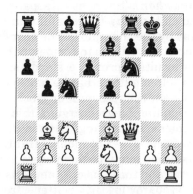

Every move counts in the position. White would love to play 13 g4 and g5 as in the game cited above, but Black's pressure on e4 is too much, e.g. 13 g4 ♗b7! 14

♗xc5 dxc5 15 g5 c4!. This is certainly not best play for White, but it does give an indication of Black's resources in the position. Even 'normal' continuations don't look particularly promising for White: 13 0-0 ♘xb3 14 axb3 ♗b7 with ...♖c8 and ...b4 to come. The pawns on e4 and c2 are usually White's biggest headaches in the Najdorf.

In view of the critical nature of the position, at this point Nigel went into the tank, and didn't emerge for 51 minutes, an amazing amount of time when one considers that he can only have been one or perhaps two moves out of his home preparation. When Short finally surfaced he produced a bizarre, but inspired, idea:

13 ♗d5   ♖b8
14 b4!?

I couldn't believe this move: it looks so ugly. The pawn move permanently weakens White along the c-file – the knight on c3 has lost its support, and if that goes then the c2 pawn is exposed. That's the minus side – and of course Short was very well aware of that. But there is method in his madness. What he is trying to do is buy himself enough time to mount an attack on the kingside: Black's pawn push to b4 is ruled out, so control over d5 is, for the time being, maintained; and forcing Black's knight back relieves the pressure on e4.

All this is being said with a great deal of hindsight. As a Najdorf devotee, I am a strong believer in Black's position and I was deeply pessimistic about White's chances at this point.

14 ...   ♘cd7
15 0-0   ♘xd5
16 ♘xd5   ♗b7
17 ♘ec3   ♘f6

Black must challenge White's control over d5 before undertaking anything else.

18 ♖ad1   ♗xd5
19 ♘xd5   ♘xd5
20 ♖xd5

Kasparov now thought for a quarter of an hour over his next move, leaving himself with just 17 minutes to play the remaining 20 moves that would bring him to the time control at move 40.

20 ...   ♖c8

Kasparov criticised this move after the game, claiming that after 20...♕c7 he would have had a large advantage. He gave a sample line the next day in *The*

Times: 21 ♕g4 f6 22 ♖f3 ♕xc2 23 ♖h3 ♖f7 24 ♕h5 h6 25 ♕g6 ♕xe4 26 ♖d1 ♔f8 27 ♗xh6 gxh6 28 ♖xh6 ♔e8 29 ♖h7 ♕c4.

Naturally, White does not need to be so co-operative, but this variation does indicate that it would not be possible for Short to play in the same *va banque* manner as the game. The problem is that White cannot really allow himself to fall back on the defensive as his queenside is so weak. For instance, 21 ♖f2 ♕c4! hits all four of the weak pawns.

21 ♕g4

Short did not hesitate before playing this bold attacking move. If he goes on the defensive, then the initiative will have passed over to Black and his attack will never get off the ground. For instance, 21 ♖f2 ♖c4!, followed by ...♕c7, and the weaknesses along the c-file begin to tell. Now the drawbacks of 14 b4 are plain to see. If the pawn were still on b2, then 21 c3 would be possible to hold up Black's play.

21 ...   f6

Forced. If instead 21...♖xc2, then 22 ♗h6 ♗f6 23 ♗xg7 ♗xg7 24 f6 wins for White.

22 ♖f3   ♖xc2

The world champion looked uncomfortable. He spent six minutes over this move, leaving himself with just ten minutes to make the remaining eighteen moves before the time control. Short, on the other hand, was

moving quickly and confidently, and at this point had just under forty minutes left.

23 ♖h3

Crude but effective: Short aims the heavy guns down at Kasparov's king.

23 ...	♖f7
24 ♕h5	h6
25 ♕g6	♔f8
26 ♗xh6	

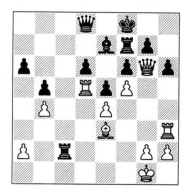

Nigel played this after little thought, resigning himself to forcing a draw – albeit in a rather spectacular manner. But why didn't he take longer over this move? He had the time (about twenty minutes) and could have at least delved into the position to make absolutely sure that there was nothing better.

Kasparov realised during the game that he would have been in trouble had White played 26 ♕h7 ♔e8 (forced) 27 ♕g8+ ♗f8, and now the move that Short had missed, 28 ♗c5!; Black cannot prevent the breakthrough on d6, e.g. 28...♕c7 29 ♖hd3! dxc5 30 ♖d8+ ♕xd8 31 ♖xd8+ ♔xd8 32 ♕xf7, with good winning chances for White.

Black can actually defend better than this. Instead of 27...♗f8, Black may play 27...♖f8, which at first glance looks disastrous after 28 ♕xg7, but he is able to launch a vicious counter-attack with 28...♕c7!. Strangely, it is White's king rather than Black's which is now in trouble; anything could happen – but with Kasparov running short of time it would be more likely to happen to him. Back to the game.

26	...	gxh6
27	♖xh6	♕b6+
28	♖c5	

It is a shame that this astonishing move is only enough to make a draw. Although it is forced anyway – 28 ♔f1 ♕f2 mate, or 28 ♔h1 ♖c1 mate – it is pleasing nonetheless.

28	...	♗d8

Giving the king an escape square.

29	♖h8+	♔e7

Now if White makes the vain winning attempt, 30 ♕g8, he comes to grief if Black just takes the rook, 30...dxc5, giving the king a flight square on d6. Instead, Short forces a draw.

30	♖h7	♖xh7+
31	♕xh7+	♔f8

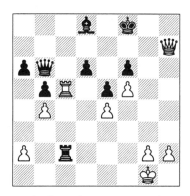

And the players agreed to a **draw**, as White has a perpetual check, e.g. 32 ♕h8+ ♔f7 33 ♕h7+ ♔f8 34 ♕h8+, etc.

A bold, aggressive game from Short, who pushed Kasparov to the brink. Nevertheless, Kasparov still leads by three clear points: 4½-1½.

Game 7

Kasparov-Short
Ruy Lopez, Anti-Marshall

I first heard the excited buzz in the press room: Princess Diana had turned up without warning to watch the match in the Savoy Theatre. It seemed an unlikely excursion, but I dashed round to check, just in case. There she was, up in the Royal Box (where else?) with Short's wife Rea, Dominic Lawson and his socialite wife, Rosa, who sold the princess jewellery at Tiffany's.

It was apparently the first recorded instance of a member of the British Royal Family ever attending a chess event. The one man in the theatre who seemed totally oblivious of this historic occasion was Garry Kasparov. He apologised afterwards for his *lèse-majesté*: 'I am very sorry. No, I didn't notice the princess. The game took too much of my concentration.'

She didn't stay long – 25 minutes on my count – but it was the most talked-about feature of the day. I was sorry to see that she had declined to use the head-set, presumably to avoid disturbing her hair, which meant that she couldn't follow the play, though Lawson kept bending down to whisper a commentary into the Royal ear. I asked Dominic afterwards if she played chess. 'I'm afraid I can't talk about that,' he said rather grandly, evidently still breathing refined air from his lofty encounter.

I happened to exit from the theatre just as she did and came across her looking remarkably shy, lonely and vulnerable as she waited on the pavement for her car to turn round and pull up. So I suppose I could have asked her the same question myself. However, I resisted the temptation to dash up for an impromptu interview in the street. My tabloid colleagues would have been disgusted at this shameful lack of professionalism.

The pop papers had not been tipped off about the visit, so they had to race round to catch up on the story, and clearly enjoyed the idea of the glamorous princess 'watching paint dry', as they put it – though, as one writer pointed out, to describe chess like that is insulting to paint.

The punsters had a field day, none more so than the *Daily Mail*, which headlined a sketch by Bill Mouland 'Diana Checks in at the Chess'. It went on: 'White Queen from W8 to WC2 keeps Short in check.

White Queen from WC2 back to W8.' Her sudden appearance at the chess, said the writer, 'was about as unlikely as Prince Charles wearing a baseball cap and munching a burger at Planet Hollywood.'

It was widely interpreted by the press as a desperate publicity boost for a tournament that was said to be costing the sponsors, *The Times*, as much as £4 million. There was much talk of money by now, the prize fund of £1.7 million attracting adverse comment, with doubts expressed as to whether Nigel Short could possibly merit the £650,000 or so he would get as the loser. The implication of much of this comment was that the players should not be paid a fortune just for enjoying themselves.

But could it really be said that were they enjoying themselves? Was Short, in particular, enjoying the public roasting he was getting as he went yet another game down? Jan Timman, the Dutch grandmaster who was beaten by Short on the way to the final, once said of the experience of playing a big chess match: 'Chess is a narrow way. I leave all pleasure behind. It is a time without pleasure. People normally go for fun, for pleasure, but chess players, through this very narrow way, try to get to God.'

Despite the encouragement of the princess's visit, Short was overwhelmed in a blistering attack by the champion from a Ruy Lopez position known as 'the Spanish torture'. Kasparov mounted a sustained attack on Short's king and broke through to an impressive victory in 36 moves. 'This was my best game yet,' he said afterwards. Michael Adams, the English number two, had seen it coming and exclaimed after move 20 at the Grandmasters' table: 'Black's getting stuffed.'

Nigel's bubble had burst once again. Leonard Barden said he would have to rethink entirely his strategy with the black pieces. Malcolm Pein, executive editor of *CHESS Monthly*, expressed his fear in the *Daily Telegraph* that the challenger was in danger of being routed. Grandmaster Julian Hodgson, the British number three, was quoted as saying: 'Nigel's trying his best, but he's just outclassed. It was a masterpiece by Kasparov.' Divinsky, the Canadian chess sage, was asked if Nigel had done anything wrong. 'Yeah,' he replied, 'he sat down today.'

The champion was pressed afterwards about the fact that the match was becoming too one-sided. 'I know people like to see a close race,' he said, 'but I am playing the world championship and I have to defend my title and I want to do it convincingly. That is my only goal. If it is not a close race, I'm sorry, but I want to win.' Nobody doubted it.

1 e4

After the embarrassment of game 5, Kasparov returns to 1 e4. He and his seconds clearly had some work to do before essaying 1 d4 again.

1	...	e5
2	♘f3	♘c6
3	♗b5	a6
4	♗a4	♘f6
5	0-0	♗e7
6	♖e1	b5
7	♗b3	0-0
8	a4	

Kasparov repeats the quiet 'Anti-Marshall' variation from games 1 and 3; it worked well enough in those, so why not again?

8	...	♗b7
9	d3	d6
10	♘bd2	♘d7

Nigel is the first to vary from Game 3. He played this move quickly and confidently – and Kasparov replied in the same manner, not wishing to concede Short the satisfaction of appearing stumped by his new move.

11 c3

This controls the key square d4, and allows the bishop to drop back to c2. The players continued rattling out their next few moves with little pause for reflection.

11	...	♘c5
12	axb5	axb5

If instead 12...♘xb3 13 bxc6 ♘xa1 14 cxb7 ♖b8 15 ♕a4, and White has a winning material advantage of two minor pieces for a rook.

13 ♖xa8

At this point Short sank into thought – which had us baffled in the commentary room: White's moves had looked natural up to this point, surely he must still have been in home preparation?

13 ... ♗xa8

The most solid continuation, keeping the queen in the centre, but in view of the mess Short soon finds himself in, 13...♕xa8 appears to be a better move. Although there is little for the queen to attack at the moment, White would always have to stay on his guard.

14 ♗c2

It seems as though White's forces are bottled up, but they possess great potential energy. Take, for instance, Black's problems if he makes the seemingly natural break in the centre, 14...d5. After 15 exd5 ♕xd5 16 d4! exd4 17 cxd4, Black cannot take the pawn on d4, because the bishop on e7 hangs to the rook on

e1, and the knight is forced to retreat to a horrible square, for if
17...♘e6, then 18 ♗b3 and d5
wins a piece.

14 ...   ♗f6

Black prevents White from
playing the pawn to d4, but Kasparov has other options.

15 b4!   ♘e6
16 ♘f1   ♗b7

Normally Black's bishop is well
placed on the long diagonal in the
Ruy Lopez, putting pressure on
the e4 pawn; but here White
hasn't pushed the pawn to d4, the
e4 point is secure, and thus the
bishop has no useful role to play.
For that reason, Short decides to
redeploy it via c8 to a more useful
diagonal. There is great similarity between this game and the
third.

17 ♘e3

An excellent square for the
knight: it might land on d5, f5, or
perhaps g4.

17 ...   g6
18 ♗b3

Now we can see the point to 15
b4: the dreaded 'Spanish' bishop
is able to return to this searing diagonal.

18 ...   ♗g7
19 h4!

The traditional way of attacking the h7, g6, f7 pawn complex.
The first world champion, Wilhelm Steinitz, was playing in exactly this way over one hundred
years ago.

19 ...   ♗c8

Continuing to re-route the
bishop, but this is too casual. I
would suggest 19...h5 instead. It
is undoubtedly risky to throw a
pawn up in front of the king like
this – White has the possibility of
prising open the position with g4
at some point but I think this is
preferable to Nigel's aimless ma-
noeuvrings over the next few
moves.

20 h5   ♔h8
21 ♘d5

The threat is 22 h6 ♗f6 23 ♘xf6
bagging the bishop pair.

21 ...   g5?

This is horrible. Both Kasparov
and Short concurred afterwards
that 21...gxh5 was the best chance,
though Black's king is in for a
rough time.

22 ♘e3

Immediately pin-pointing the
shortcomings of Short's last move:
the f5 square is a chronic weakness in Black's camp.

22 ...   ♘f4

Maybe Short had been relying

on this sally to hold his position together, but Kasparov thought for less than a minute before playing ...

23 g3

...cutting the Gordian knot: Black can have the pawn on h5, but this only opens the h-file, at the end of which stands Black's king.

23 ...   ♞xh5

24 ♞f5

Jonathan Speelman thought that Black was 'busted' at this moment, and what follows bears this out, though there were many who thought that the simplest way for White to continue was 24 ♔g2, threatening 25 ♖h1. In the Grandmaster's analysis room the following variation was mooted: 24 ♔g2 g4 25 ♞h2 (25 ♞h4 looks just as good to me) 25...♞f6 26 ♖h1 ♛d7 27 ♞f5 ♞e7 28 ♞xg7 ♔xg7 29 ♛d2 ♞g6 30 ♛h6+ ♔h8 31 ♞f1, with the unstoppable threat of 32 ♗g5, and White crashes through on h7.

24 ...   ♗xf5

25 exf5   ♛d7

Compared to the variations we had just been looking at, this position didn't appear to be quite as clear. If now 26 ♞xg5 ♞f6 27 ♛f3 d5! and Black is fighting back.

26 ♗xg5!

Kasparov obviously had it all worked out. If 26...♛xf5, then 27 ♗d5! wins material, for example: 27...♛d7 28 ♞h4 ♞f6 29 ♗xf6 ♗xf6 30 ♛f3; or 27...♞d8 28 ♗e7

♖e8 29 ♞h4 ♛d7 30 ♗xd8 ♛xd8 31 ♛xh5.

So Black cannot win the f5 pawn. But before we are blinded into thinking that Kasparov has, once again, played a perfect game, it should be pointed out that Short could have put up a much stiffer resistance if he had played 26...♞f6 in this position, with the idea of 27 ♞h4 d5. White must be preferred because of the bishop pair, but cut and dried it is not. It would seem that 24 ♔g2 was more convincing.

26 ...   h6?

Giving White a whole tempo.

27 ♞h4   ♞f6

28 ♗xf6   ♗xf6

29 ♛h5

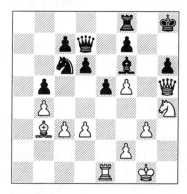

White has given up the bishop pair, but his queen has found its way over to Black's weakened kingside. White's attacking prospects are actually improved by the fact that there are opposite-coloured bishops on the board. In order to diminish the force of an attack it is necessary to exchange off pieces, but how is it possible to remove the bishop on b3? It is this piece that is the key to White's attack in so many variations.

29 ...   ♔h7
30 ♘g2

The knight needs to be re-deployed and this turns out very well, though later Kasparov criticised the move. He recommended instead 30 ♘f3, so that after 30...♘e7 31 d4! opens up the position for the bishop and rook (Black cannot take on f5 because of ♗c2 setting up a lethal pin).

30 ...   ♘e7
31 ♘e3   ♘g8

Bringing the knight over has shored up a few holes around the king, and it is not obvious to see how White will continue the attack. Having played his last few moves at speed, Kasparov now sank into thought, filling those of us supporting Short with some optimism. Had the world champion blown his chances?

32 d4!?

A move typical of Kasparov's style: just when it seems as though his initiative is fading, he finds a way to keep the position fluid. This pawn break opens the e-file for the rook, as well as the b1-h7 diagonal for the bishop.

32 ...   exd4
33 cxd4   ♗xd4?

With about eight minutes left to reach move forty, Short characteristically grabs a pawn and

hopes for the best. Perhaps Kasparov's reply was difficult to see because it was not of the 'crash, bang, wallop' kind, but merely moved another piece into the attack. Kasparov indicated afterwards that 33...♗g5 was the only way to put up a defence.

34 ♘g4

Surprisingly there is no answer to White's threats. The move which ought to hold up the attack is 34...♗f6, but that runs into 35 ♕xh6+ ♘xh6 36 ♘xf6+ ♔g7 37 ♘xd7, winning a piece. Otherwise, White will play 35 f6, for instance: 34...♕d8 35 f6! ♗xf6 36 ♗c2+ ♔g7 37 ♕f5 ♖e8 38 ♕h7+ ♔f8 39 ♖xe8+ ♕xe8 40 ♕xg8+ ♔xg8 41 ♘xf6+, with a winning endgame.

34 ...   ♔g7
35 ♘xh6!

If now 35...♘xh6 36 ♕g5+ ♔h7 37 f6, threatening ♕g7 mate as well as ♗c2+ winning.

35 ...   ♗f6
36 ♗xf7!

It is fitting that this bishop – the Spanish bishop – should deliver the killer blow: its influence has been felt through the whole game without it ever coming into direct contact with the opposing forces – until now. If 36...♖xf7 37 ♕g6+ and ♕xg8 mate; likewise 36...♘xh6 37 ♕g6+ ♔h8 38 ♕xh6 mate, so **Short resigned**.

A splendid game from Kasparov. He played the first part in the style of his arch-rival Karpov, patiently manoeuvring and building up an attack, and finished it off like the old Kasparov with a dynamic and unexpected pawn sacrifice, which unmasked a lethal attacking potential in his forces.

Kasparov has now won three Ruy Lopez games in very similar style: a slow build-up from the opening, outmanoeuvring Short in the middlegame, then turning on the heat between moves 30-40. Although one cannot talk of Kasparov's brilliant opening preparation – he is still avoiding a theoretical discussion on the Marshall Gambit – it is becoming clear that he has analysed Short's entire style and pin-pointed certain weaknesses. He even hinted at this in the Channel 4 interview after the game: 'Nigel does not feel comfortable when he has no clear plan, when he has to manoeuvre his pieces on the back rows.'

The score: 5½-1½ to Kasparov.

Game 8
Short-Kasparov
Sicilian Najdorf

The morning of Thursday, 23 September, opened with a sensation. Short had lost his chief coach, Lubomir Kavalek, who had decamped in mysterious circumstances to the United States. Michael Stean, Short's manager, sought to reassure everyone: 'He has gone home for family reasons and he will be back.' Kavalek himself was quoted as saying: 'I have no plan at the moment to return to London, but eventually I might.'

Both statements were greeted with scepticism in the press room, where it was generally believed the two had fallen out over Short's conduct of the match. There was also a persistent rumour, never confirmed, that there had been a disagreement over money. Kavalek had told someone after the seventh game: 'I feel very sorry for him. The match should not have been like this. It didn't need to be so bad.'

Kavalek, who had escaped to the United States from Czechoslovakia after the 'Prague Spring' had been crushed by Soviet tanks, was credited with putting backbone into Short for his matches against Karpov and Timman. He had introduced more aggression into his play and a healthy dislike for Russians. The effect on the challenger of losing the man who had been described as his 'Svengali' at such a crucial time was incalculable.

It then became known that Short had been struggling on in secret without his chief mentor since the third game. The Spanish arbiter, Carlos Falcon, had noticed that Short appeared distressed when he shook hands with him before the fifth game and had passed on the traditional greeting: 'I wish you good luck from your second, Lubosh Kavalek.' This had evidently bothered Short at the time and the arbiter was asked not to repeat the greeting.

Short must have been seriously inconvenienced by Kavalek's departure. His other main supports were the German grandmaster, Robert Hübner, who had once played Kasparov in a match himself, and Jon Speelman, who was busy writing about the match and appearing on television as a member of the Channel 4 commentary team. Kasparov, in contrast, had his full set of coaches, including formidable former Soviet grandmasters of the calibre of Alexander Belyavsky and Zurab Azmaiparashvili.

The champion had had mysterious problems of his own with his coaches in previous matches against Karpov, when suspicions arose as to whether one of them had supplied some of his opening plans to his opponent. Now, however, all seemed to be running smoothly at the Regent's Park house he was using as a training camp.

After the news about Kavalek it was possible to look back at Short's disastrous fourth game defeat and understand why he had played so badly. His skilful preparation for the fifth game also had to be seen in a new and even more surprising light. In former world championship matches it would have been possible for him, in a situation like this, to call a time-out to put his house in order. The rules for this match, however, with the tightly organised television schedules and ticket sales, made this impossible.

With the news of his coach's departure breaking to the media on the eve of the eighth game, it must have been very hard for Short to play. In the event, he did well enough to draw, albeit playing with the white pieces. At a key moment in the game, when Kasparov took an hour over move 14, a grandmaster commented on Nigel's response: 'He looked as though he had been shot.' In the event, he survived, but he was now losing by six points to two, taking the champion half-way, in less than three weeks, to retaining his title.

1	e4	c5
2	♘f3	d6
3	d4	cxd4
4	♘xd4	♘f6
5	♘c3	a6

Both players are prepared for a fight: Short feels most comfortable with double-edged, attacking positions where his objectives are clear, while Kasparov enjoys the counter-attacking possibilities which will present themselves.

6	♗c4	e6
7	♗b3	♘bd7
8	f4	♘c5

So far, everything is the same as game 6, but now Short varies from his previous 9 f5.

9 e5

This aggressive thrust was first played and analysed by the Ukrainian grandmaster Adrian Mikhalchishin, so it must be well known to the Kasparov camp. The idea is to open up lines against Black's king with great speed, hoping to catch it with a quick attack, particularly as Black has hardly any pieces developed. The drawback is that after ...

| 9 | ... | dxe5 |
| 10 | fxe5 | |

... White's e-pawn is isolated from the rest of its pawn chain, and could turn out to be a weakness. So, the battle-lines are drawn: White must hope that his attack breaks through or he will stand worse due to his inferior pawn structure.

10 ...   ⚞fd7

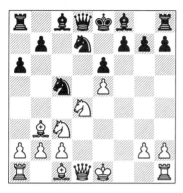

11 ⚝f4   b5

It looks suicidal to ignore the development of his kingside, but at the moment this is the best thing to do. For instance, 11...⚝e7 12 ♕g4! 0-0? 13 ⚝h6, winning material. In other words, Black's king is just as safe in the centre as on the kingside, so he may as well do something about his queenside forces which for the moment are badly bottled up.

12 ♕g4

Previously, 12 ♕e2 had been played in a couple of games, but Short's move is much more aggressive, aiming at the e6 pawn as well as g7.

12 ...   h5!?
13 ♕g3   h4
14 ♕g4

Kasparov thought for eight minutes over 12...h5, and a further five over 13...h4, perhaps indicating that he was not totally familiar with the position. At the post-game press conference Kasparov revealed that he had briefly analysed this move a couple of years ago with Anand – but can that really be the extent of his preparation for this wild position? On the basis of how the game turned out, and the length of time he was taking on these opening moves, I would say, yes: he gave every appearance that he was improvising – which is really chancing it.

Throwing the h-pawn up the board has little point to it unless followed up by ...

14 ...   g5

... over which Kasparov thought for forty minutes; he now had less than an hour to make the required forty moves.

The chaos starts here. First of all, let's take a look at what would happen if White captures the g-pawn: 15 ⚝xg5? ⚞xe5!, when White has nothing better than to go in for 16 ⚝xd8 ⚞xg4 17 ⚝g5 ⚝b7, and I would prefer to play Black because of the centre pawns and excellent diagonals for the bishops. Likewise, 15 ♕xg5 ♕xg5 16 ⚝xg5 ⚞xe5 is slightly better for Black.

However, if we had any pessimistic thoughts about Nigel's position, they were dispelled when we found 15 0-0-0!, with the idea 15...gxf4 16 ⚞xe6! ⚞xe6 17 ⚝xe6 fxe6 18 ♕xe6+ with a crushing attack; Black has many ways to attempt a defence, but it is one-way traffic. And after a fifteen minute think, Short played it.

15 0-0-0!

However, Kasparov thought for just a couple of minutes before playing:

15 ...   ♕e7!

The ending after 16 ♕xg5 is now more palatable for White as his king is already castled, though this would hardly be a triumph for his opening. Instead Short thought for half an hour and came up with:

16 ♘c6!   ♘xb3+
17 axb3   ♕c5

White must give up a piece, but naturally it is all planned.

18 ♘e4   ♕xc6
19 ♗xg5   ♗b7
20 ♖d6!!

Short got up from the board and left Kasparov sitting in agony. He stared at the board in disbelief, shaking his head, disgusted that he had overlooked

this tremendous move. After the game he admitted that he thought he was lost at this moment.

If he plays 20...♕xe4 21 ♖xe6+ is crushing; or 20...♘xe5 21 ♘f6+ ♔e7 22 ♖hd1!, and if 22...♘xg4 23 ♖d7+ mates.

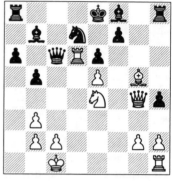

20 ...   ♗xd6
21 ♘xd6+   ♔f8
22 ♖f1   ♘xe5
23 ♕xe6   ♕d5

Black's queen covers f7 by 'X-ray'.

24 ♖xf7+

It seems as though it is all over: Kasparov's king is laid bare, exposed to a vicious assault from White's remaining pieces. But from this moment on, the world champion shifts gear: if before his play had been hesitant and he appeared uncomfortable, he now visibly regained his composure – perhaps he felt that the outcome of the game was no longer in his hands – and he began to play with authority and confidence. The next ten moves he banged out instantly, putting all the pressure back on Short.

24	...	♘xf7
25	♗e7+	♔g7
26	♕f6+	♔h7
27	♘xf7	

White threatens 28 ♕h6+ and 29 ♕g6 mate; as well as 28 ♘g5+ and 29 ♕g6 mate. There is only one move that prevents both.

27	...	♕h5
28	♘g5+	♔g8
29	♕e6+	♔g7
30	♕f6+	♔g8

Short repeats the position here, and at move 33, as he was beginning to run a little short of time. As a result of Kasparov moving so quickly, Nigel had had no opportunity to think during his opponent's time.

31	♕e6+	♔g7
32	♗f6+	♔h6

Side-stepping 32...♔g6 33 ♗e5+ ♔xg5 34 ♕f6+ ♔g4 35 h3 mate.

33	♘f7+	♔h7

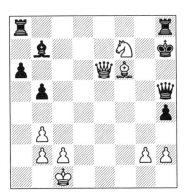

34 ♘g5+
After the game both players

considered that 34 ♘xh8 was winning, but later Kasparov found a miraculous defence. The main variation runs: 34...♖xh8! 35 ♕e7+ ♔g6 36 ♗xh8; now if 36...♖xh8 37 ♕xb7 is a winning endgame for White, but 36...♕g5+! 37 ♕xg5+ ♔xg5 38 g3 hxg3 39 hxg3 ♔g4! 40 ♗e5 ♗d5!! 41 ♔d2 ♔f3! 42 ♔c3 ♗e4! and White is unable to create a second passed pawn on the queenside. A curious position: I must admit that I had to stare at it for some time before I convinced myself that White could make no progress.

34	...	♔h6
35	♗xh8+	

Probably the best winning chance. 35 ♕e7 was suggested instead, but it seems as though Black may defend himself in a similar way to the previous variation: 35...♖ag8! 36 ♘f7+ ♔g6 37 ♘xh8 ♖xh8 38 ♗xh8 ♕g5+ 39 ♕xg5+ ♔xg5 etc.

35	...	♕g6

The only move. If instead 35...♔xg5 36 ♕e5+! ♔g4 37 h3 mate; or 36...♔g6 37 ♕f6+ ♔h7 38 ♕g7 mate. Beautiful.

36	♘f7+	♔h7
37	♕e7	♕xg2

Kasparov cracked this pawn off, relieved that he was finally getting a sniff of White's king, though it transpires that it might actually be a blunder. Instead the bizarre-looking 37...♔g8! saves the day for Black, for instance: 38 ♘e5? ♕h7!; or 38 ♕xb7 ♖f8! 39

♘e5 ♖f1+ 40 ♔d2 ♕d6+ 41 ♘d3 ♔xh8, with a probable draw.

38 ♗e5

With less than five minutes left to get to move forty, and his king suddenly under attack, Short plays it safe, moving his threatened bishop and defending the h-pawn. While everything in White's camp is guarded, Kasparov may now deliver perpetual check.

38 ♗d4!, preventing the perpetual check by controlling some key squares, is a serious winning attempt. If Black checks randomly: 38...♕f1+ 39 ♔d2 ♕g2+ 40 ♔c3 ♖c8+ 41 ♔b4 a5+ 42 ♔a3 b4+ 43 ♔a2, the king finds refuge – and then it is White's turn to attack again. There are many complicated variations, and I'm not even sure that one could say unequivocally that Black was lost, but it would have been a severe test for Kasparov.

38	...	♕f1+
39	♔d2	♕f2+
40	♔d3	♕f3+
41	♔d2	♕f2+

There is no escape from the checks, so the players agreed a **draw**.

An excellent attacking game from Short, but perhaps Kasparov's defensive play was even more impressive. There were several occasions when it seemed that resigning was a sensible option, but Kasparov moved quickly and, on the whole, accurately, avoiding the many traps in the position. Perhaps Short did have a win somewhere along the line, but even with the benefit of a great deal of hindsight it is still not entirely clear, and finding it over the board proved impossible.

The score: 6-2 in Kasparov's favour.

Game 9

Kasparov-Short
Nimzo-Indian Defence

When Short slumped to his fifth defeat in the ninth game, visibly downhearted as he conceded after 52 moves, one commentator noted that 'the play is ceasing to have any sporting significance and is becoming more of an exhibition for the champion.' This was typical of much negative comment on the match. Some of the criticism, inspired by rivals wishing to damage *The Times*, was plainly hostile. Others, provoked by what they regarded as the massive 'hype' of the sponsors, poked gentle fun at the idea that chess could ever be exciting or fun. The fact that the great British hope was trailing so badly gave more fuel to the detractors.

One of the strongest swipes came in the *Independent* in an article by William Hartston headlined 'Paper is Mated by its own Hype'. He claimed that the sponsors 'did not understand what they were buying' and that the match had been a commercial disaster. He cited the vaunted Predict-a-Move service, which had attracted only 2,000 calls for the first three games against the projected 20,000 calls a day, and had finally been axed. He claimed that the first month's genuine ticket sales were only about 600 of the 26,000 on offer. 'The chess-playing public recognise hype when they see it,' he added.

He concluded this blast with the observation that Ray Keene was due to name an elephant at London Zoo. 'It would be appropriate,' he said, 'if it were large, white and named *The Times* World Chess Championship.' The inevitable counter-blast came, not from *The Times*, where one might have expected it, but from Dominic Lawson in the *Daily Telegraph*, who accused Hartston of perpetuating a personal feud with Keene that went back to their days at university.

The consensus in the Grandmasters' room was that Hartston was right about the 'hype', which had made Short's failure all the more of a let-down. Hartston was not alone in his comments. The London *Evening Standard*, which had been disappointed in a bid of its own to sponsor the match, published what is known in the trade as 'a knocking piece', claiming that 'all the tricks known to the promotion of boxing were applied to chess', but to no avail: there was 'no bloodshed, no giggles and no fun.'

It also targeted Keene personally, exuding a strong whiff of sour grapes: 'The chess establishment is making hay while the sun shines, but, it seems, only those who are friends, relatives or protégés – as most of it is – of Raymond Keene. Those on whom the man smiles are in the commentary box, acting as PRs and on the reception desk. Keene himself has at least four books riding on the match.' The article concluded: 'As for the game itself, well, it had its moments, but unfortunately it had its hours too, and the hours came first.'

One writer likened the chess to Pinter, whose new work, 'Moonlight', had just opened in London: 'The script is pure Harold Pinter. Or Samuel Beckett: six hours of silence and body language, with an ending that no-one expects or understands.' The match was certainly, as Simon Barnes put it, 'a matter of great silences and minute gestures.' And, like the central figure in the new Pinter play, Nigel Short appeared to be on his death-bed.

Some of the growing hostility to the match was more deeply rooted, based on a principled objection by many senior British players to Short's breakaway from FIDE, which they saw as opportunistic and mercenary and not in the best interests of the game. The fact that he was losing so badly only added insult to injury. John Nunn, a leading English grandmaster, was conspicuously absent from the match, evidently as a personal protest. Asked about this, he said: 'The thing you have to understand about chess players is that they are individualists, often with big egos. They devote their lives to a game and then you find they start playing games with their lives.'

Even *The Times*, which had gone out of its way to keep the challenger's hopes alive in the minds of the public – likening him, rather implausibly, in one piece to Nigel Mansell ('This could yet be remembered as the year of the two Nigels') – began to lose heart. It headed its report on the ninth game: 'Challenger Paralysed by the Power of Kasparov's Mind'.

Short had evidently tried to repeat the successful opening he had used in the fifth game, but this time Kasparov was ready for it. According to Leonard Barden, when the champion saw Short's tenth move, 'he raised his eyebrows and smirked. His twelfth move stunned Short, who pondered for 46 minutes before replying.' To make things worse, Short had missed a chance of a draw. After three weeks, the challenger was back on the rack.

1	d4	♘f6
2	c4	e6
3	♘c3	♗b4
4	♕c2	

Kasparov shows a willingness to repeat the variation from game 5, where Short made a draw with ease using prepared analysis. One would have thought that a danger sign would start flashing in the challenger's head; but ...

| 4 | ... | d5 |

On seeing this move, the world champion gave a smile like a crocodile who had just spied a lamb gambolling innocently by the river bank. Kasparov and his team of analysts have such a fearsome reputation that getting involved in a theoretical discussion struck those of us watching as being more foolish than brave. It was still not too late to vary with 4...0-0 or 4...c5, both of which are reasonable moves.

5	cxd5	exd5
6	♗g5	h6
7	♗h4	c5
8	dxc5	g5
9	♗g3	♘e4
10	e3	♕a5
11	♘e2	

Here it is, the big improvement. At first sight the knight move appears clumsy, for although its comrade on c3 is given some additional support, the bishop on f1 is blocked in. At any rate, Short appeared unimpressed and quickly played:

| 11 | ... | ♗f5 |

Setting up some nasty threats based on a discovered attack against White's queen.

| 12 | ♗e5 | |

Played instantly. In the Channel 4 studio Jonathan Speelman, one of Short's seconds, squirmed uncomfortably in his seat: he admitted that no one in the team had considered this move. Short was now on his own.

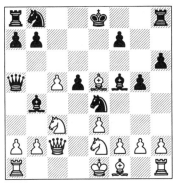

| 12 | ... | 0-0 |

Played after 42 minutes. The next day, the chief arbiter, Yuri Averbakh, commented to me that if anyone thinks for more than twenty minutes over a move, then the result is bound to be a blunder. There is more than a grain of truth in the remark. After a while variations just spin round in one's head and it is no longer possible to think clearly.

I suspect that is what happened to Short here. He selects a safe, but uninspired, option, thereby avoiding the most critical variations, but not presenting

Kasparov with any particular problems.

However, given the complexity of the position, it was hardly surprising that he became a little confused; Kasparov said that he and his team had worked for many days on the position without coming to a definite conclusion.

The most obvious moves to try are those which attack White's queen. Unfortunately, they are not terribly good: 12...♘g3 13 ♕b3, and Black's rook in the corner can still be taken; or 12...♘xc3 13 ♕xf5 ♘e4+ 14 ♔d1, and it is actually White who has the better attacking chances.

12...f6 looks the soundest move; then 13 ♗xb8 ♖xb8 14 ♘d4, and now the modest retreat 14...♗d7!, as suggested by the *Daily Telegraph* correspondent Malcolm Pein, is perhaps Black's best option.

12...♗g6!? is crazier, with the idea that if 13 ♗xh8 ♘xc3, and now 14 ♕xc3!? ♗xc3 15 ♗xc3 is a far from silly queen sacrifice.

No wonder Nigel short-circuited – I have barely touched upon the possibilities in the position and I'm getting confused.

| 13 | ♘d4 | ♗g6 |
| 14 | ♘b3 | |

Short has an unpleasant choice before him: either retreat the queen, losing the initiative; or transpose into an ending a clear pawn down. After almost twenty minutes thought he chose the latter.

If 14...♕d8 15 ♗d3!, and Black, still a pawn down and facing a strong attack on his king (how he wishes he hadn't moved his g-pawn!) could go down without a fight.

14	...	♘xc3
15	♗xc3	♗xc2
16	♘xa5	♗xc3+
17	bxc3	b6

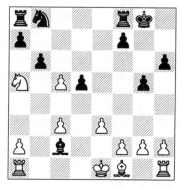

Although a pawn down, Short has a chance to save the position because his development is slightly better. After the game Kasparov revealed that he had had this position on his board at home, and considered that both 18 ♔d2 and 18 ♘b3 gave good winning chances – he had truly taken revenge for being out-prepared in game 5. 'I said I would do my homework!' he chuckled on the Channel 4 interview afterwards.

| 18 | ♔d2 | bxa5 |
| 19 | ♔xc2 | ♖c8 |

20 h4!

The weakness of ...g5 coming home to roost.

20 ...   ♞d7

21 hxg5   ♞xc5

21...hxg5? 22 ♖h5 f6 23 ♗a6 ♖c7 24 ♖ah1 is dreadful for Black.

22 gxh6   ♞e4

Short has some counterplay, but Kasparov finds some precise moves to consolidate his advantage.

23 c4   ♞xf2

24 ♖h4!   f5!

The only move to keep going. If instead 24...♞e4 25 ♖d1 is the end.

25 ♖d4!   dxc4

26 ♗xc4+   ♚h7

27 ♖f1   ♞g4

28 ♚d2   ♖ab8

If instead 28...♞xh6 29 g4! with the idea 29...♞xg4 30 ♗e6; or 29...fxg4 30 ♗d3+ ♚g8 31 ♖f6 ♞f7 32 ♖xg4+ ♚f8 33 ♖gf4 ♖c7 34 ♗c4, winning material.

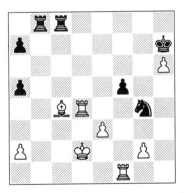

Short has done well to struggle on this far, but the last variation

is indicative of the problems he now faces: his king has no pawn cover, and could, if he is not careful, become exposed to attack. Moreover his remaining pawns are chronically weak; and the long range bishop is better than the knight.

29 ♖xf5   ♖b2+

30 ♚d3   ♖xg2

31 ♗e6   ♖c7

32 ♖xa5   ♞f2+

33 ♚e2   ♖h2

34 ♚f3   ♞h1

Humiliation.

35 ♖d7+!   ♖xd7

36 ♗xd7   ♚xh6

37 ♖xa7   ♚g5

38 ♖a5+   ♚f6

39 ♗c6   ♖c2

40 ♖f5+   ♚e7

41 ♗d5   ♚d6

42 ♖h5   ♖d2

Until this moment Kasparov's technique has been good: he has controlled the game, quelling Short's counterplay and gradually simplifying down to a winning

position. But with his next move
he begins to slip. It was clear from
the way that both players were
rattling out their moves that they
both considered the result beyond
doubt, but that is when careless-
ness sets in. 43 e4! ♘f2 44 ♔e3
♖b2 45 ♖h6+, driving the king to a
poor position, was a more certain
way of finishing off the game.

43	♖xh1	♖xd5
44	a4	♖a5
45	♖a1	♔e5
46	e4??	

An appalling error. 46 ♖a3 still
wins if White is careful, e.g.
46...♔f5 47 e4+ ♔e5 48 ♔e3, and
either king or rook must retreat;
or 46...♔d5 47 ♔f4 ♔c4 48 e4.

46 ...   ♔e6??

46...♖c5 would have drawn:

(a) 47 ♖a3 ♖c4 48 a5 ♖xe4 49 a6
♖f4+ 50 ♔e3 ♖f8 51 a7 ♖a8, followed by marching the king over
and taking the pawn;

(b) 47 a5 is more complicated:
47...♖c3+ 48 ♔g4 ♔xe4 49 a6 ♖c8
50 a7 ♖a8 51 ♖a5 ♔d4 52 ♔f5 ♔c4
53 ♔e6 ♔b4 54 ♖a1 ♔c5 55 ♔d7
♔b6 56 ♖b1+ ♔c5! (56...♔xa7 57
♔c7! and ♖a1 mate) 57 ♖b7 ♖h8
and the position is drawn, for if 58
♖b8 ♖h7+ wins the pawn.

47	♔e3	♔d6
48	♔d4	♔d7
49	♔c4	♔c6
50	♔b4	♖e5
51	♖c1+	♔b6
52	♖c4	

And **Black resigned**.

The rook remains on c4, cutting
off Black's king, and White's king
marches round and ferries the e-
pawn to the eighth.

A tremendous psychological
blow for Kasparov, refuting Short's
opening, even though the game
was marred by a mistake at the
end.

The score: 7-2 to Kasparov.

Game 10

Short-Kasparov
Sicilian Najdorf

Things did not look up in the tenth game, even though Short raised the watchers' hopes with a startling queen sacrifice that appeared to give him numerous chances of a win. The consensus in the Grandmasters' room was that the challenger had seemed afraid to win. One of them said: 'If he can't win that, he can't win anything.' The official bulletin even asked cheekily if Short had seen fit to take William Hill's odds against him winning a single game.

Malcolm Pein was scathing in the *Telegraph*: 'Nigel Short missed win after win last night as he followed up a brilliant queen sacrifice with one of the most blunder-filled sequences ever seen in a world championship.' Barden said Short had 'let slip another commanding position'. Keene said Kasparov 'rose from the dead'. The general view was the Short had snatched a draw from the jaws of victory.

Short's hesitant showing in this game was the last straw for many people, who felt he had been given the benefit of too many doubts. Professor G. Spencer-Brown wrote an exasperated letter to the *Telegraph* in which he attacked Short's performance as 'a disgrace', 'dismal', 'inept' and 'the worst performance of any contender in any world chess championship'.

It was left to Dominic Lawson, as ever, to rush to his friend's defence. 'Professor Spencer-Brown is, I understand, a psychologist and it is interesting to speculate on the psychological motives of those who rush into print to claim that they would have won games which Short has only drawn. The reason, I submit, is that it is a wonderful way for such people to feel that, in some sense, they are actually better calculators than the strongest British chess player of the twentieth century. They can, for one brief, chest-puffing, self-deluding moment, portray themselves as better at chess than Nigel Short.'

Again Lawson referred to Short's *'enemies'*, rather than his critics, and hinted that the challenger might be consulting libel lawyers. Many of the comments being directed against Short, it seemed to me, were not motivated by enmity at all, simply by disappointment that he seemed, rightly or wrongly, not to be playing to his full potential. It was rather like the football fans' rage at Graham ('Turnip') Taylor for the failures of the England team. That, too, was destined to reach a peak before the chess match was over.

Chess can set off violent emotions in players and spectators alike, which seems strange in such an outwardly pacific game. But chess is basically an image of war, and the trumpets of war are never distant from a world championship. Simon Barnes attempted to explain this phenomenon: 'Each contestant aims to destroy the other: that is what all games are about. Short and Kasparov are not seeking to create beauty, or wonderful intellectual patterns, or to reach that strange landscape where games and mathematics and even music combine. No. They are trying to win. That is the beginning and end of it. The point is the ultimate simplicity of victory. Or defeat, of course.'

By game five Nigel Short appeared to have lost his initial fear of losing. By game ten, however, he had apparently failed to conquer an even more insidious inhibition: the fear of victory.

1	e4	c5
2	♘f3	d6
3	d4	cxd4
4	♘xd4	♘f6
5	♘c3	a6
6	♗c4	e6
7	♗b3	♘bd7
8	f4	♘c5
9	♕f3	

The first deviation from their previous match games. This early queen move makes castling long a serious option.

9 ...   b5

After fifteen minutes thought.

10 f5   ♗d7!

When White's queen stands on f3 in the Sicilian, it is usual that Black places his bishop opposite, on b7. Here, however, with White making an early assault on the e6 square, the bishop is better placed on d7. The immediate point of the move is to prevent White from playing the knight into c6.

11 fxe6

This capture does not look correct. It is impossible to put more pressure on the e6 pawn, so it was better to leave the pawn on f5 as a possible spearhead for an attack.

11	...	fxe6
12	♗g5	♗e7
13	0-0-0	

Played after an agonising 52 minute think. During that time, the more we looked at the position the less we liked it for White and Short must have been thinking the same. The two pawns on e6 and d6 prevent White's knights from penetrating, and at any moment Black may take the bishop pair.

13	...	0-0 *(D)*
14	e5!?	

If White does not attempt some quick action he will stand worse, for the reasons given above. Short's move is, however, a gamble, and

he was aware of that at the time, hence the brooding over 13 0-0-0.

The coming queen sacrifice he was happy with, but the problem was that in this position he saw no answer to 14...♘d5!; the best that White has is to play 15 ♗xe7 ♘xe7 16 ♕e3 d5!. The bishop on b3 is locked out of the game and Black has good attacking chances on the queenside. It is an indication of how bad the alternatives were that Short considered this his best option when examining his 13th move.

14 ...   ♘fe4

Kasparov admitted afterwards to being lulled into a false sense of security by Short's long cogitation at move 13, and he failed to appreciate the strength of the queen sacrifice. Otherwise he would surely have contented himself with 14...♘d5, guaranteeing a promising game.

15	♗xe7	♕xe7
16	♘xe4!	♖xf3
17	exd6	♘xb3+
18	♘xb3	♕f8

19 gxf3

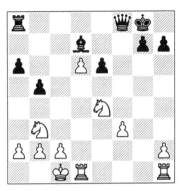

The flurry of tactics has produced a position in which Short has rook, knight and pawn for Kasparov's queen. Normally, such a material balance should not favour the pieces, but here the pawn on d6 is so powerful that it is actually White who has the upper hand.

Kasparov considered that his position was lost at this point. Perhaps he was being too gloomy. 19...♗c6 would have put up a better defence than the game, with the idea of playing the bishop to d5 to cut off the rook's support.

19	...	♕xf3
20	♘ec5	♗c6
21	♖he1	e5
22	d7	

One step closer.

22	...	♖d8
23	♖d6	a5!?

Kasparov knows that his position is lost, so he starts to make as much trouble as possible. The aim of this move is to break the co-ordination of White's pieces in the hope that something will drop off.

Short's reply is safe and strong, and in view of his time shortage probably most prudent, but I still do not see why the pawn cannot be taken: 24 ♘xa5 ♕f4+ 25 ♔b1 ♕b4 26 ♖ed1 ♗f3 was given by Kasparov afterwards, assessing the position as unclear, but why not 27 ♘c6? Then I see no defence for Black.

	24	a3	a4
	25	♘d2	♕g2
	26	c3	

Giving the king an escape square. Now Short can go for the kill.

	26	...	♗d5
	27	♘d3	♗b3

Kasparov continues to play in 'swindle mode'. The bishop sets up mating threats, preventing the knights wandering too far.

At this point Short had eight minutes left to reach the time control at move forty, while Kasparov had 25 minutes.

	28	♘xe5	♕xh2 *(D)*
	29	♘c6!	

This should win by force; but with Short having just five minutes left, Kasparov stepped up the pressure by making his moves almost instantly.

	29	...	♕xd6
	30	♖e8+	♔f7
	31	♘xd8+	♔g6
	32	♘e6	

Short could have simplified the

position by playing 32 ♖e6+ ♗xe6 33 ♘xe6 ♕xe6 (or 33...♕xd7 34 ♘f8+) 34 d8♕. While this position must be winning, it will still be necessary to play some accurate moves to finish off – Black's h-pawn could still be a problem – and with just a few minutes left Short decided to go for a 'cleaner' kill.

	32	...	♕h2
	33	♘f4+	

It has been suggested that 33 ♖f8 was a clearer winning move, but after 33...♕h4! Black is still thrashing around, and I do not see how White continues. For instance, 34 ♘xb3 ♕e1+ 35 ♔c2 axb3+ 36 ♔d3 ♕d1+ actually wins for Black.

	33	...	♔h6
	34	♘d3	♕g1+!

Short had used up most of his time in reaching this position, convinced that Black had no move. He now discovered that his intended 35 ♘e1 loses to 35...♕g4 (threatening mate on d1) 36 ♘xb3 ♕xd7!.

Although he still has a winning position, I felt that from this moment Short was not going to do it. Missing this fiendish trap threw him; now into his final minute, his brain froze, unable to calculate.

35 ⦿e1 ♛g5

The simplest win is 36 ⦿h1+ ♚g6 37 ♘e5+ ♚f5 38 ♘c6. The d-pawn promotes on the next move.

36 ♘e5

Now it's more tricky, and with practically no time left, downright problematic.

36 ... g6

37 ⦿f1

37 ♘c6! wins beautifully after 37...♛f5 38 ♘e4 ♛xd7 39 ⦿h1+ ♚g7 40 ⦿xh7+! ♚xh7 41 ♘f6+. That's just for the record – it is impossible to see with nothing on the clock.

37 ... ♝e6
38 ♘f7+ ♝xf7
39 ⦿xf7 ♛d5

White now has a similar win to the previous variation: 40 ♘e4 ♛d3 41 ⦿f2!! (threatening 42 ⦿d2)

41...♛xd7 42 ⦿h2+ ♚g7 43 ⦿xh7+ ♚xh7 44 ♘f6+.

40 ⦿e7

Short made the time control with just four seconds to spare. Having been clearly thrown at move 34, it was a miracle that he had made the forty moves at all, let alone found a win, and having got there, that he still had a playable position.

40 ... ♛d6
41 ⦿f7 ♛d3!

The d-pawn is still on the verge of promotion, but to force it through would involve taking the knight away from defending the king, leaving it exposed to checks from the queen. Short is simply relieved to have any kind of position left after the time scramble and forces a draw.

The saddest picture was of the white queen which Short had placed at his side of the board during the time scramble, ready to make a queen, still standing there at the end of the game.

42	♘e4	♛e3+
43	♘d2	♛d3

And the players agreed a **draw**.

In the Channel 4 TV interview immediately after the game he admitted: 'At the end I did not have it in me to play on. I can even lose such a position if I try too hard. Maybe a draw is the correct result anyway.' He looked absolutely shattered.

Kasparov, on the other hand, was delighted. He must now believe that he can risk almost anything and still get away with it. There was general admiration for the world champion's resourcefulness in a position which looked beyond hope. In the words of Australian Grandmaster Ian Rogers, 'Kasparov makes Lazarus look like an amateur.'

The score: 7½-2½ in Kasparov's favour.

Game 11

Kasparov-Short
Scotch Opening

Meanwhile, back in Moscow, the growing crisis between Boris Yeltsin and the Russian Parliament was reaching a violent showdown. There was speculation that Kasparov would be put off his game by the bloody events back home. He said little about this at the press conferences, saying merely that he had every confidence that Yeltsin was doing the right thing. His manager, Andrew Page, told me that the champion was staying in touch with events, but saw no cause for alarm, since Yeltsin seemed to be on top of things.

Short, doubtless at Kavalek's instigation, had made great play of Kasparov's Communist affiliations in some pre-match statements that were now looking rather naive. I had defended Kasparov against these charges in the *Daily Telegraph*, saying that, far from being a Kremlin stooge, he had been viewed with the gravest suspicion, and was gratified to receive support in a letter from the former KGB defector, Oleg Gordievsky.

He wrote: 'Donald Trelford is right to say that Moscow had doubts about Garry Kasparov. When Mr Kasparov visited Britain for the first time in 1983, the KGB station in London, where I was working, was swamped by alarmist sounding cables from headquarters. They contained instructions to spy on all movements and statements of the young chess player and to report immediately on all "suspicious circumstances" connected with him and his "surroundings". Moscow wanted to know what he was saying publicly, whether he was critical of his opponent Karpov, and whether he was dropping any hints about the role of the Communist Party and the Soviet State. I had little doubt that Mr Kasparov was an independent, nonconformist and even rebellious individual.'

I thought of these machinations at the Russian embassy when the ambassador, Boris Pankin, turned up to see the match and visited the Grandmasters' room. Gordievsky's testimony is significant and appears to bear out Kasparov's own belief that the Soviet chess authorities at that time, through their links with the KGB, were trying to find grounds to disqualify him from the world championship cycle that resulted in his challenge to Karpov in the following year. As Nikolai

Krogius, the chess official on the Soviet Sports Committee, had told him: 'We've got one world champion. We don't need another.'

Kasparov turned up late for the next game, which was interpreted as over-confidence. More likely, it was caused by a traffic jam. If it *was* a mark of supreme confidence, it was shared by the bookmakers, who were quoting Short's chances at 150-1 – longer odds, as Leonard Barden pointed out, than against the discovery of the Loch Ness monster! Whatever the reason for the delay, the clocks had already started before he sat down to make the opening move as White.

The Times described the scene at the Savoy Theatre in a faintly disapproving tone (the champion was, after all, late for an event that was costing them a great deal of money): 'Kasparov, wearing a smart business suit, burst onto the stage, shook hands, sat down and made the first move all in one brisk movement. It was as though he had just arrived from the airport and was fitting in a quick game of chess before a much more important engagement elsewhere.'

Short, meanwhile, had been sitting at the chessboard fiddling with his hands and wondering what to do, 'wearing a sports jacket and tightly knotted tie that made him look like a gangling schoolboy.' Was this gamesmanship by Kasparov, giving the impression that he didn't need to try very hard, in order to humiliate his opponent, or was it just an accident? Keene took the view that it was 'psychological warfare'.

If it was, it didn't succeed, for despite an unexpected Scotch opening by the champion, Short managed a draw on move 50 when there were insufficient pieces left on the board for either player to win. In the endgame the Grandmasters thought it was Kasparov who was fighting for the draw. He admitted afterwards: 'I am very tired. We are fighting in every game. There are no time-outs and we are playing a faster time-control than in any previous world championship match.'

Maybe, it occurred to me, that remark provides a clue to his late arrival: could it be that the champion simply overslept?

1 e4	e5
2 ♘f3	♘c6
3 d4	

The Scotch cannot have come as a surprise to Short. Kasparov successfully employed this relic from the nineteenth century in his 1990 world championship match against Karpov, proving that there were still a great many undiscovered possibilities.

3 ...	exd4
4 ♘xd4	♗c5
5 ♘xc6	

A slight surprise. Theoretical debate has centred on 5 ♗e3 in the last couple of years.

5 ...	♕f6

The approved response. White must contort himself in order to defend f2, and only then does Black capture the knight.

6 ♕d2   dxc6

Short places piece activity higher than pawn structure. 6...♕xc6 has been played before, but in that case White is able to use the d5 square for a knight.

7 ♘c3   ♗e6
8 ♘a4!?

This is Kasparov's new idea. It looks outlandish to put the knight out at the side of the board, but somehow it pays off.

8 ...   ♖d8

I'm sure Nigel would really have liked to castle queenside, but, unfortunately, that one is illegal.

9 ♗d3   ♗d4
10 0-0   ♘e7?!

Not an incisive move. For Nigel's improvement see game 17.

11 c3

Kasparov thought for almost half an hour over this move, though he revealed after the game that he had already analysed this exact position in his preparation; no doubt he was just checking the tactics in the complex variations that arise after 11 c3.

Black's bishop does not have a good square to retreat to. If 11...♗b6, then simply 12 ♘xb6 axb6 13 ♕e2!, followed by advancing the f-pawn; or 11...♗e5 12 f4 wins. Instead, Short opts for an ending – which is also fairly miserable.

11 ...   b5
12 cxd4   ♕xd4
13 ♕c2!

A tremendously strong move.

13 ...   ♕xa4

The best of a bad choice. Instead:

(a) 13...♕xd3 14 ♕xd3 ♖xd3 15 ♘c5 is very pleasant for White in spite of being a pawn down – the knight on c5 is untouchable;

(b) 13...bxa4 14 ♗e2 and the bishops will reign supreme.

14 ♕xa4   bxa4
15 ♗c2

There were many people watching who considered that Black's position was already lost, though with hindsight this judgement was too pessimistic. Nigel likes grabbing material, and after the game he made it clear that he thought his position was quite tenable. Kasparov admitted to being 'too optimistic, I was looking for something that was not there.'

Indeed, from this moment on, it was Kasparov who spent more

time over his moves, while Nigel played quickly and confidently. Although a pawn up, Black's queenside pawns are a mess, and the bishop pair can be a lethal weapon. Moreover, White's kingside pawn majority has great potential.

15	...	&c4
16	&e1	&b5
17	&e3	♘c8
18	&c5	♘b6
19	&ad1	&xd1
20	&xd1	a6
21	f4	♘d7
22	&a3	

The bishop looks good here, scything across Black's king, but Short soon blunts its force. 22 &d4 was perhaps stronger with the idea 22...f6 23 e5, breaking the position open for the bishops.

22	...	h5
23	&f2	&h6
24	e5	c5!

At a stroke Short improves his co-ordination and hinders Kasparov's. As well as cutting out the bishop, the pawn move allows the rook to swing across into play, and sometimes the bishop may drop back to c6.

25	&f5	&b6
26	&d2	g6
27	&c2	&e6
28	&g3	♘b6!

Breaking out at exactly the right time, before the king comes marching in, and just as Kasparov is running out of time. At this point he had just over ten minutes left to reach move forty, whereas Short had half an hour.

29	&xc5	♘c4
30	&d5	♘xb2
31	f5	&c6!

Kasparov had obviously missed this one, and looked disgusted with himself for not making more of his advantage.

32 &d2

Simplifying the position with 32 &d8+ might have been more prudent in view of the time situation: 32...&xd8 33 fxe6 &d5! 34 exf7 &xf7 35 a3. The position should be a draw, though Black must be a little careful. I suspect that Kasparov was still thinking of winning when really he has lost his advantage and ought to be steering the game to a draw.

32	...	gxf5
33	♔f4	♘c4
34	♖e2	f6!
35	♗xf5	♖xe5
36	♗d3	♗d5

Nigel's pawns are terrible – split, isolated and doubled – but he does have two more of them than his opponent, so by now the advantage has swung in his favour.

37 ♗d4

Kasparov's hubris keeps him playing for the win, but he ought to have played 37 ♗xc4! ♗xc4 38 ♖xe5+ fxe5+ 39 ♔xe5 ♗xa2, reaching an ending where he is two pawns down, but because of the bishops of opposite colour the position is drawn.

37	...	♖xe2
38	♗xe2	♔e7
39	♗xh5	♗xg2
40	♗d1	

Kasparov was down to his final minute, but even so, this was not an impressive move. 40 ♗e2 ♗d5 41 ♗c5+ ♔e6 42 a3, safeguards the a-pawn and guarantees the draw.

40 ... a3!

Fixing the pawn on a light square enabling the bishop to attack it. Now Short is definitely playing for the win.

41	h4	♗d5
42	h5	♘e5
43	h6	♗xa2

Setting up an amusing trap. If 44 h7 ♗b1 45 h8♕ ♘g6+; or 45 h8♘!? a2, and there is nothing to stop the king marching over and capturing the knight, resulting in a position with excellent winning chances for Black.

| 44 | ♗c5+ | ♔f7 |
| 45 | ♗c2 | ♗c4 |

After this White can force a draw. In order to maintain any winning chances Black must play 45...♘g6+, but after 46 ♔e3 ♗c4 47 ♗xa3, I cannot believe that it will be too difficult to defend: the h-pawn is still a problem, and the bishops cope easily with Black's split pawns.

46	h7!	♔g7
47	♗f8+	♔h8
48	♗e7	♗d3
49	♗xf6+	♔xh7
50	♗xe5	♗xc2

And the players agreed a **draw**. White simply marches the king to a1, and can even give up the bishop for the c-pawn.

In spite of a poor opening, this was a more confident performance from Short who fought back well from a difficult position.

Afterwards Kasparov looked visibly tired, perhaps as a result of his Herculean defence in the previous game. Can Short take advantage of it in his next game?

The score: 8-3 in Kasparov's favour.

Game 12

Short-Kasparov
Sicilian Najdorf

So far in the fourth week Short had fought back with two strong draws. The experts were beginning to talk about a 'mini-revival'. The Savoy Theatre was noticeably fuller on the Saturday than for some time, perhaps because people hoped to be present at that long-awaited moment when the Englishman finally won a game. Alas, it was not to be, though the audience broke out in spontaneous applause as the players made it three draws in a row.

What the audience were applauding was an intense tactical exchange leading to an exciting endgame which grandmasters thought was well played on each side. Kasparov said afterwards: 'There is a lot of psychology in this type of match. The kind of chess we are playing is unusually ferocious and intense for a world championship match.'

Speelman praised Short's performance, saying it had been 'his best week. He has matched the champion blow for blow and if he can put past disappointments behind him he has a good chance of finally winning a game.'

A different picture of the challenger's prospects emerged over the weekend, however, as grandmasters were quoted in the press as saying that Short's campaign was 'on the verge of collapse'. The *Sunday Times*, itself part of the sponsoring Murdoch empire, ran a headline: 'Short "Near to Collapse" as His Chess Camp Feuds'. The story went on: 'Short began the championship as David fighting Goliath: he is now being compared with Eddie "the Eagle" Edwards, Britain's skiing no-hoper.'

It claimed Short had thrown away so many opportunities to win or draw games that his preparation was clearly defective, casting doubt on his backroom team. With Kavalek gone, he had been forced to rely on Hübner and Speelman, neither of whom could spare him enough time. Some critics. it said, 'fear he may be so badly affected that the championship could end his career. Others claim that his performance is an embarrassment.'

Murray Chandler, editor of the *British Chess Magazine*, put some of the blame on Lawson. 'I think Dominic Lawson is probably brighter than me in 99 per cent of the things he does, but when it comes to beating Kasparov you have got to be somebody who knows how to do it. It is not about waffle and bullshit. It's about playing the moves on the board.'

Lawson insisted that he was not providing technical advice and dismissed the complaints as sour grapes and jealousy. Short wrote to the paper in defence of the friend who had defended him so often. Grandmaster Tony Miles, never one to mince his words, dismissed the friendship as 'mutual social climbing'. Of Short's play, he said simply: 'He is out of his depth. Having said that, most people would be – against Kasparov.'

1	e4	c5
2	♘f3	d6
3	d4	cxd4
4	♘xd4	♘f6
5	♘c3	a6
6	♗c4	e6
7	♗b3	♘c6

Kasparov is the first to vary from previous games in the match where he played 7...♘bd7.

8	f4	♗e7
9	♗e3	0-0
10	♕f3	

Short signals his intention to castle on the queenside, but Kasparov sets his counterplay going before it gets there.

10	...	♘xd4
11	♗xd4	b5

Black plans ...♗b7 and ...b4 with an attack on the e4 pawn. It is possible to prevent this with 12

a3, but after 12...♗b7 Black is doing well because the centre is immobilised. Short decides to take action before getting pinned down.

12	♗xf6	♗xf6
13	e5	♗h4+
14	g3	♖b8

Kasparov was still bashing his moves out, which must have been a little disconcerting for Short. Afterwards he said that he knew that this piece sacrifice was a recommendation of the Grandmaster Shamkovich, but he couldn't remember any of the analysis. So much for the great memories of chessplayers.

It is possible for White to bail out here by playing: 15 0-0-0 ♗b7 16 ♘e4 ♗e7 17 exd6 ♗xd6 18 ♕d3 ♗xe4 19 ♕xe4, with a level position. However, it is not in Short's nature to back down from a fight, and he accepts the sacrifice.

15	gxh4	♗b7
16	♘e4	dxe5
17	♖g1	

Clearing the rook from the long diagonal and setting up threats against g7 makes sense. If Black now plays 17...♕xh4+, then 18 ♕g3! ♕xg3+ 19 ♘xg3 exf4 20 ♘h5 g6 21 ♘xf4 gives White the better endgame.

17 ...   g6

This, apparently, is a new move and shows the depth of Kasparov's opening preparation. It is an extraordinary move. A piece down for just one pawn, it would seem that Black should be continuing the attack to get compensation; but in the middle of the chaos, he takes time out to make a quiet defensive move.

18 ♖d1   ♗xe4

The super-subtle 18...♕e7 was recommended by American GM Joel Benjamin with the idea of 19 ♕e3 exf4 20 ♕xf4 ♕b4+, though I'm not convinced that Black's position after 19 ♕e2 is better than the game.

19 ♕xe4   ♕xh4+
20 ♔e2

Kasparov thought for 35 minutes over his next move. He was at the crossroads: should he keep the queens on and play against White's exposed king; or go for an ending in which he could push his pawns down the board? He plumped for the latter, but had to admit after the game that he made the wrong decision. Having said that, 20...exf4 21 ♖g2 is quite playable for White. Kasparov was understandably worried that if he ever tried to advance his pawns, then his king would be vulnerable to attack with queens on the board.

20 ...   ♕xh2+
21 ♖g2   ♕xf4
22 ♕xf4   exf4
23 ♔f3   ♖fd8

Keeping the f4 pawn is impossible: 23...e5? 24 ♖g5 ♖be8 25 ♖e1 and ♖xe5.

24 ♖xd8+   ♖xd8
25 ♔xf4

Opinion was divided over who stood better here, with the majority on the side of the pawns. However, the more we looked at the position, the more we liked Nigel's chances. Four connected pawns can be powerful, but it takes four times longer than usual to move them down the board. Kasparov's next move is an admission that caution is necessary on Black's part.

25 ...   ♟f8

An excellent move. We' had all been considering the 'natural' 25...♟g7, though in many variations White was able to penetrate with a rook, or sometimes even transfer the king to the queenside. Moving the king across to e7 is directed against that, as well as being ready to blockade a passed pawn, should White be able to create one.

26 ♞e3

Unfortunately for White, he must waste a move before advancing on the queenside because of ...ℚd4+.

26 ...   ♞e7
27 c4   h5
28 a4

The race is on. Black charges down the kingside, while White hastens to create a passed pawn on the opposite flank.

28 ...   bxa4
29 ♝xa4   h4
30 c5   ℚh8
31 ℚc2

The best place for the rook – behind the passed pawn.

31 ...   h3
32 ♝c6!   e5
33 ♞f2   h2
34 ℚc1   a5!

Preventing possibilities such as b4 and ♝b7 winning the a-pawn.

35 ♝d5

This has been criticised for allowing Black's rook into the game, but it is difficult to suggest alternatives. For instance, if 35 ♝h1 f5 36 c6 e4!, cutting out the bishop.

35 ...   ℚd8
36 ♝g2   ℚd2+
37 ♞g3   ♞d7
38 ℚa1

Heading straight for the draw. Instead 38 c6+ ♞c7 39 ℚe1!? appears dangerous because of 39...f6 40 ♞xh2 ℚxb2 41 ♞g3, and the rook is ready to hassle White's king. However, 39...♞d6! 40 ♞xh2 f5! intending to cut off the bishop with ...e4 is still drawn.

38 ...   f5
39 ♞xh2 ℚxb2
40 ℚxa5   e4

Here Short offered a **draw** which Kasparov accepted immediately. A plausible conclusion might be 41 ♞g1 ℚc2 42 ℚa6 ℚxc5 43 ℚxg6, with a drawn position.

The score: 8½-3½ in Kasparov's favour.

Game 13

Kasparov-Short
Slav Defence

The fourth week of the match opened amid growing speculation that Short would be put out his misery as soon as Kasparov had retained his title, which was now seen as a formality. But the sponsors would hear none of it, arguing that the 24-game format had been agreed in advance and was part of the rules. They made it seem like a doctor insisting that a course of antibiotics must be completed in full even after the flu symptoms have gone. Kasparov's camp let it be known, however, that the champion would not be averse to playing a speed chess challenge over the last few games, once the result had been settled, in order to popularise this version of the game with the large television audience.

The *Daily Telegraph*, however, had reached the end of its tether and wrote a devastating leader calling for the match to be called off, saying it was 'more than flesh and blood could bear'. It was headlined 'Sheer Embarrassment' and began: 'If it gobbles like a turkey and tastes like a turkey, it seems a reasonable assumption that it is a turkey.' It went on to say the match 'now inspires the sensations that cause sensitive pet owners to decide that it would be kinder to have the poor creature put down. Nigel Short is not only British: he is a sympathetic and decent man whom we were proud to claim as our own chess columnist. This makes it all the more painful to see him mauled thrice weekly by the lions in a half-empty coliseum.'

Game 13 proved no luckier for Short than what had gone before, but at least he managed to draw with Black after what a Grandmaster called 'a brilliant display of tactical fireworks'. Kasparov regards thirteen as his lucky number, having been born on 13 April and becoming the thirteenth world champion, and always asks for it whenever he can as his room number in hotels around the world.

On this occasion he seemed distracted and admitted afterwards: 'Obviously the events in Moscow took some of my attention. In fact, I have spent more time watching CNN than looking at the chessboard. It's a distraction and it's upsetting because lots of people died.'

As the televised scenes of the bloody assault on the White House in Moscow came up in the press room, the chess writers too were distracted.

One of them, a foreigner of a philosophical turn of mind who had often come up to me before, said suddenly and rather dramatically:

'Can you give me any hope?'

Not quite knowing what he meant, I replied: 'Do you mean about Nigel?'

'No,' he said, pointing at the screen, 'I meant about the world.'

'That's rather easier to be hopeful about,' I said. 'I can see Yeltsin finishing off his enemies, but I can't see Nigel finishing off Kasparov.'

1 d4   d5

There is general relief that Nigel decides not to continue the battle of home analysis in the Nimzo-Indian Defence.

2 c4   c6

Short has never before played the Slav Defence, and in view of Kasparov's excellent record as White against this opening (11 wins, six draws, no losses) there were many who thought this was not the right moment for its debut. Nevertheless, I think Short's choice was good. Too often Kasparov's opponents have been caught out by his painstaking opening preparation, so to frustrate him by 'running' from a theoretical discussion has to be good psychology.

3 ♘c3   ♘f6
4 ♘f3   dxc4
5 a4

Preventing Black from protecting the pawn on c4 with ...b5.

5 ...   ♗f5

Black develops the bishop before playing the pawn to e6 to avoid blocking it in.

6 e3   e6
7 ♗xc4   ♗b4

It is the weakening of the b4 square which makes the position playable for Black: it gives him a vital toe-hold for his pieces in the enemy camp.

8 0-0   ♘bd7
9 ♕e2

Kasparov has also played 9 ♘h4 in this position, using it to defeat one of the young pretenders, Vishy Anand from India. He has also employed 9 ♕e2 before, envisaging a sharp pawn sacrifice which Short quickly declined.

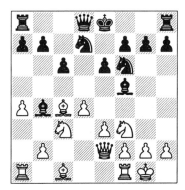

9 ...   ♗g6
10 e4   0-0

One of Kasparov's opponents captured the pawn – 10...♗xc3 11 bxc3 ♘xe4 – though had cause to regret it later. White gains excellent compensation in the form of the two bishops, starting with 12 ♗a3 preventing Black from castling kingside.

11 ♗d3   ♛a5

White's central pawns are not as powerful as they might appear at first sight. Black's pieces exert formidable pressure on them, and there is little that White can do to prevent ...c5 breaking them apart. Therefore, Kasparov feels compelled to take action in the centre before his opponent.

12 e5

This is a trade: Black gains a superb square for his knight on d5, as does White on e4.

12 ...   ♞d5
13 ♗xg6   fxg6

This recapture is essential. If 13...hxg6 14 ♞e4, with the idea ♞fg5 and ♛f3-h3-h7 mate, is hard to meet in a sensible manner. Anyway, taking with the f-pawn is not so daft: the f-file can be a source of counterplay for Black.

14 ♞e4   c5!

Breaking down White's centre.

15 ♞d6

Until this moment Short had been moving quickly, but now he went into a think – he was clearly at the end of his home preparation.

In the Channel 4 studio, we were having difficulties solving the problems of the position. 15...cxd4 16 ♞xd4 ♞c5 17 ♛g4 is not at all appetising for White;

while protecting the b-pawn with the grovelling 15...♖ab8 is hardly in the spirit of the position, and anyway, not Short's style.

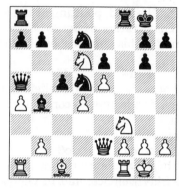

15 ...   ♛a6!?

An original idea. Normally, doubled and isolated pawns are frowned upon, for the simple reason that they cannot protect themselves, but here the weakness of Short's pawn structure is compensated for by the activity of his pieces.

16 ♛xa6   bxa6
17 ♞g5

Kasparov criticised his own move afterwards saying that he believed 17 ♗e3 would guarantee him a clear advantage – which Short disputed. It is a shame that they were not to debate the position in a following game.

17 ...   cxd4
18 ♞xe6   ♖fb8

The white knights are terribly imposing, but Short has worked out a good defence in advance.

19 ♖d1   ♞xe5

20 ☖xd4

Kasparov now expected the continuation 20...♗xd6 21 ☖xd5 ♘f7. Although not absolutely clear, White has the better chances due to his dominating pieces and superior pawn structure. Instead Short finds a way to exchange off Kasparov's active pieces.

  20 ...   **☖b6!**
  21 ☖xd5   **☖xd6**
  22 ☖xd6

Not 22 ☖xe5 ☖d1 mates.

  22 ...   **♗xd6**
  23 ♗f4   **☖e8**
  24 ♘d4   **♗c5**

Although Short has weak a-pawns, he also has some targets to aim for himself, namely the pawns on f2 and b2, and his pieces are more active than White's. Conclusion: Kasparov has made nothing of his advantage of the white pieces.

  25 ♘b3   **♗b4**

A poor move. It is necessary to keep the b-file open with 25...♗f8. For instance if White plays as in

the game with 26 ♗e3 then 26...☖b8! is strong; and meanwhile 26...♘d3 or 26...♘c4 are potent threats. White should draw by picking up the a7 pawn, but that is all he can hope for.

  26 ♗e3   **♘d3**
  27 ☖b1   **☖c8**
  28 ♗xa7

Why not grab the pawn? None of us watching could see a reason not to, but as it turns out, we (and Kasparov, I might add) were wrong again. Instead, 28 ♘d4, keeping the rook from c2, would preserve some chances for White – because of Black's weak pawns – but whether it would be enough to win is another matter.

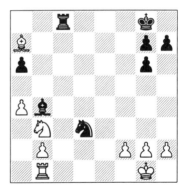

  28 ...   **☖c2**
  29 ♗d4

It seemed as though Kasparov had got his cake and was about to eat it. The bishop defends both weak pawns and Black's pieces cannot improve their positions. Short, however, has seen further.

  29 ...   **♔f7**

30 h3   ♗e7!

Realising that the bishop is White's key defensive piece, Short simply intends to exchange it off. After it goes, then both the f2 and b2 pawns will hang.

Instead of falling back on the defensive, Kasparov decides to force a draw.

31 ♖d1   ♘xb2
32 ♘a1   ♘xd1

Not 32...♖e2 33 ♔f1 ♘xd1 34 ♔xe2, and the knight is trapped.

33 ♘xc2   ♗f6

34 ♗xf6

And Kasparov offered a **draw**, which Short accepted in view of the continuation 34...gxf6 35 a5 ♘b2 36 ♘b4 ♘c4 37 ♘xa6 ♘xa5, with a barren position.

Another good day for Nigel. He neutralised Kasparov's early initiative and forced a draw. He finally looks as though he is playing in the same league as the world champion.

The score: 9-4 in Kasparov's favour.

Game 14

Short-Kasparov
Sicilian Najdorf

The smell of meat and burgundy is unmistakable as you go through the swing doors at Simpson's-in-the-Strand. Straight ahead is the downstairs restaurant, the room used to launch the match and choose the colours, which was once known as the Great Divan, where chess players of the nineteenth century gathered to play and smoke a cigar. Now the waiters in white aprons down to their ankles push their silver wagons from table to table, unrolling the lids to reveal saddles of lamb and barons of beef. Posters about the chess are everywhere.

Brian Clivaz, the tail-coated manager, moves from room to room talking about the chess, for he is a great *aficionado*, following the monitors showing the state of the game or talking with authority in the Grandmasters' room in the bar downstairs. 'This is the Mecca of the mind,' he has been quoted as saying. 'What can be the point of a restaurant like this if it's just to shovel out plates of food to tourists and businessmen? It's our purpose here to encourage the intelligentsia. Wine, good food, chess: they all go together.'

The grandmasters have a large table with a notice firmly discouraging anyone from sitting down who is of lesser standing than an international master. On the table are two chessboards on which up to a dozen or so itinerant experts make the moves the players are thinking about in the theatre. As they do so, they shout to each other cheerfully, knock someone's idea on the head with a laugh or offer a variation. As they do all this, their comments are recorded on a lap-top computer which taps out the official bulletin. Alongside them is a smaller table, no less important, laden with plates of sandwiches to feed their motor minds.

In the room is a bar and a set of tables at which people watch the monitors and play the moves on their hand-held chess sets. There is a table in one corner at which old chess books, many rare and valuable, are offered for sale by a man who appears to be wearing an RAF tie. You can tell the state of a game as you walk in. If it's heading for a boring draw, the mood is down. If it's nearing the time-control, or if either player has made an innovative or surprising move, the buzz can be heard half-way up the stairs.

Two floors up is the ornate press room, with its computer screens, telephones and television monitors. Every move is shouted across the room. A waiter brings round beer and sandwiches. Telephone calls are made in nearly every known language. When Leontxo Garcia is dictating his copy to *El Pais* in Madrid, it seems impossible that anyone could take it down at such speed. I've seen Garcia's shaven bald head at chess tournaments from Leningrad to Dubai. His assistant brightens up the room each day with exotic clothes, her skirt slashed nearly to the waist.

There was a sense of anticipation in the press room during game 14 as Short patiently built up what seemed to be a winning position. Would this finally be the day he made the long-awaited breakthrough? He was playing White and people expected big things from the challenger. There was an expectant mood in the Grandmasters' room, too, as they saw him seize an early initiative.

Suddenly, it all turned sour on Short's move 34, which was greeted with a cascade of incredulous boos by the experts. Short admitted afterwards that it was 'very stupid' and Kasparov maintained that the right move then could have beaten him. After that the champion seemed to have the advantage, which made it all the more surprising when he offered the draw. Short grabbed it eagerly, knowing that his winning chances had gone.

The Times, always ready to give the challenger the benefit of the doubt, was in no doubt about this game: 'He lost his nerve.'

Why, then, did Kasparov offer the draw? 'I wasn't in the right mood' was his uncharacteristic reply. Having been let off the hook, he settled for what he had got, thankful for the small mercy Short had granted him. The grandmasters were still puzzled. 'As far as I can tell,' said one, 'this is the first instance in the match where the game ended well before the play was exhausted. Let's hope this doesn't become a trend. Kasparov has admitted to being tired, but his stated match strategy of playing for a win with White and going for the win with Black only if it falls in his lap is not going to sit well with the public.'

1	e4	c5
2	♘f3	d6
3	d4	cxd4
4	♘xd4	♘f6
5	♘c3	a6
6	♗c4	e6
7	♗b3	♘c6
8	♗e3	♗e7

9	f4	0-0
10	0-0	

Short is the first to deviate from game 14 where he played 10 ♕f3, though it didn't stop both players rattling out their replies until move 17. The line has been well known since the early 1970s, and Kasparov has even written about it in an openings survey.

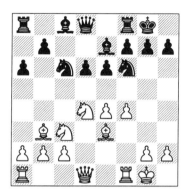

10 ...   ♘xd4
11 ♗xd4   b5

As in game 14, Kasparov strives to attack White's centre straight away with ...b4 and ...♗b7, and just as in that game, Short is forced to advance.

12 e5   dxe5
13 fxe5   ♘d7
14 ♘e4   ♗b7

White's build up appears impressive, but Black has a compact position which is very hard to crack.

15 ♘d6   ♗xd6
16 exd6   ♕g5

This position has been seen several times before in master games. Kasparov and Nikitin, writing in *Sicilian ...e6 and ...d6 systems* (Batsford) in 1982, recommend that White plays 17 ♖f2 here, saying that 'The fundamental danger for White lies not in the direct threat of mate at g2, but in the advance of the e- and

f-pawns, which will significantly fortify Black's attacking potential.'

The further progress of the game bears out their assessment exactly.

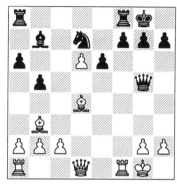

17 ♕e2

Short chooses to ignore Kasparov's advice which, as one might expect, set the world champion thinking.

17 ...   e5

This is the theoretically approved move, most players of the white pieces now preferring to retreat their bishop to e3 – with negative consequences. Take for instance Browne-Donner from 1974: 18 ♗e3 ♕g6 19 ♖ad1 ♔h8 20 h4 f5! 21 h5 ♕f6 22 a4 f4! with a strong attack brewing on the kingside.

18 ♗c3

This is more purposeful than 18 ♗e3. Short evolves a plan of pushing his queenside pawns.

18 ...   ♕g6
19 ♖ad1   ♔h8

Kasparov is playing consequent chess. His last two moves enable him to throw his f-pawn up the board. White cannot play 20 ♗xe5 because of 20...♖ae8 winning a piece.

20 ♗d5   ♗xd5
21 ♖xd5   ♕e6
22 ♖fd1   ♖fc8

The players were unaware that they were actually following the game Christiansen-Spasov, Indonesia 1982 – a tournament in which my co-commentator on Channel 4, Raymond Keene, was actually participating. Ray's normally elephantine memory let him down on this occasion, for he couldn't remember the game at all, though he did offer a plausible excuse: 'Most of Spasov's games were over before people sat down,' a reference to the Bulgarian's habit of agreeing quick draws and hitting the beach. Instead of 22...♖fc8, Spasov played 22...f5, but that seems poor on account of 23 a4 bxa4 24 ♖a5, when the whole of Black's queenside might drop off.

With the rook on c8, 23 a4 runs into 23...bxa4 24 ♖a5 ♖c6, holding the a-pawn and hitting the d-pawn.

23 ♗a5   ♖c6
24 b3   ♖ac8?

Carelessly wasting a whole move: Kasparov plays the rook to e8 to support the e-pawn on the very next turn.

25 ♗c7

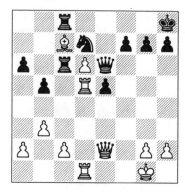

Manoeuvring the bishop to c7 is a double-edged idea. If Black's knight is ever dislodged then the bishop is in the perfect place to shepherd the d-pawn to the queening square; if the knight remains there, however, then the bishop could just look offside, miles from the action on the kingside.

25 ...   ♖e8
26 c4

Setting in train the queenside pawn majority.

26 ...   bxc4
27 bxc4   f5

Having secured his queenside, Kasparov finally gets around to pushing his kingside pawns.

28 h3   h6

Both players take time out to create an escape square for their kings in the event of a check on the back rank, but I think this favours Black more than White. It would have been better to chug round with the queen straight away.

29 ♕c2   e4
30 ♕a4

It was essential for White to try and dislodge the blockaders, otherwise the c- and d-pawns are going nowhere.

30	...	**♖c5**
31	**♖xc5**	**♘xc5**
32	**♕c6**	**♘d7**

Over at the Grandmasters' analysis room we were examining the consequences of 32...♘d3, which is not clearly bad for Black, and certainly gives good hacking chances. Years of playing against Karpov has taught the world champion that playing cautiously has its merits too, and he therefore keeps the d-pawn securely blockaded.

33 ♕d5

Centralising the queen and clearing the path for the c-pawn to fly down the board. Black cannot contemplate exchanging queens because there would be nothing to stop the c-pawn marching to promotion – so he must pin his hopes on his kingside counterplay. By this stage we were very much more optimistic about Short's position.

33	...	**♕g6** *(D)*
34	**♕d2?**	

Short said afterwards: 'This was a very stupid move. For a moment I lost my sense of balance. My first intention was to play 34 c5, but then I saw a variation which lost and I simply decided to play safe. The problem is that in this position there are no safe moves, you just have to keep going.'

Spot on, Nige. A great many trees had to be felled in the days following the game for Kasparov to try and prove that he wasn't actually losing this position, but I see that as moot: in a situation as complicated as this, one would never expect best play, particularly as both players were running low on time. 34 c5 simply had to be played, whatever the consequences.

For those of you interested, here is a résumé of the analysis so far after 34 c5:

(a) 34...f4 35 c6 f3 36 g4 f2+ 37 ♔xf2 e3+ 38 ♔g1! wins for White; or 35...♘f6 36 ♕c4 f3 37 ♕f1! holds the fort long enough for White to push the pawns;

(b) 34...♖e5 35 ♕a8+ ♔h7 36 c6 ♖b5! (this was Kasparov's improvement on 36...♖c5 which he had considered during the game). Now the most amazing line which Kasparov gave was 37 cxd7 ♖b2 38 g4 fxg4 39 ♕e8 ♕f5 40 ♕f8 (40 ♖f1 ♕c5+ 41 ♔h1 ♕c2 wins the point of playing the rook to b2 and not c2) 40...♕xf8 41 ♖f1 ♕g8

42 d8♕ ♕xa2 43 d7 (covering the h2 square with the bishop) 43...gxh3 44 ♕h8+ ♔xh8 45 d8♕+ ♔h7 46 ♕d6 ♖g2+ 47 ♔h1 ♖g6 48 ♕h2 ♕g2+ 49 ♕xg2 hxg2+ wins.

After 36...♖b5, Kasparov believed that 37 ♕xa6, bringing the queen back to f1 to defend would lead to a draw, while Jonathan Speelman recommended 37 ♔h1, so that g2 could be defended by the rook.

So, it is too early for a definite conclusion to be reached and my deadline approaches. Back to the game, where Kasparov quickly assumed the upper hand.

34 ...   ♖e5

Preventing the pawn from moving forward.

35 ♕e3   ♕e6

This is good for Black, but 35...♕f7, threatening ...♕xc4 and ...f4, is even stronger.

36 ♖c1   ♖c5
37 ♖c2

So that if 37...♖xc4 38 ♕b3. Therefore Kasparov brings the king round to defend the queen.

37 ...   ♔g8
38 a4   ♔f7
39 ♕f2   e3

And here, quite uncharacteristically, Kasparov offered a **draw** which Short accepted instantly. There is no doubting Kasparov's advantage: White's pawns on the queenside are blocked, while Black's on the kingside are mobile; moreover, White's bishop looks completely out of play if the pawns aren't moving. When asked immediately after the game why he had offered the draw, Kasparov replied: 'I didn't see a clear win, so enough is enough.' But if he had had more energy and motivation then he would have been looking harder for it. He appeared extremely tired.

The score: 9½-4½ in favour of Kasparov.

Game 15
Kasparov-Short
Queen's Gambit Declined

Perhaps all Kasparov needed was a good night's sleep, for he emerged from this weary mood on the Thursday to win with White in what the experts called 'a clean kill'. 'A packed audience,' said Keene, 'thrilled to Kasparov's sparkling technique.' So much in chess at this level turns out to be about motivation and energy.

And yet, if the general public were asked to name the most important quality in a chess champion, they would probably say 'brains'. It is by no means clear, even to doctors, what kind of brain is needed. The owner may or may not succeed in normal academic pursuits; some champions have been conventionally clever, others less obviously so. It was once said of the American prodigy, Samuel Reshevsky, that he was 'living proof that you could be a world champion with an IQ of less than 100.' An American psychologist reported the case of a mentally retarded inmate at an institution for 'congenital idiots', as it was then called, who could beat people of normal intelligence over the chessboard.

Psychologists have tried many experiments to pin down the mental characteristics of a chess champion. They have generally concluded that the essential talent is an exceptionally high level of visual and spatial intelligence, which is traced to the left-hand side of the brain. Conventional intelligence comes from the other side of the brain. Over the years a chess champion like Kasparov is thought to build up a mental encyclopaedia containing up to 100,000 significant chess patterns – comparable, according to one estimate, with the number of words in Shakespeare's vocabulary.

What has never been adequately measured is the degree to which characteristics such as 'courage' can affect these mental equations. For Kasparov, whose attitudes were moulded in the trauma of his first marathon battle against Karpov over the winter of 1984-85, courage – or, as he usually calls it, 'fighting spirit' – means a great deal. When he was five games down and on the brink of defeat, he used to play the songs of Vissotski, Russia's Bob Dylan, in his ear to give him the inspiration to go out and play.

The tone of these poems may be gauged from this extract, which Kasparov quotes at the beginning of his autobiography:

'You can take an easier route,
But we chose one that is the most difficult
And dangerous like a path of war.'

Many of Vissotski's songs are in the same heroic vein. One wonders what songs could be found at this late stage to inspire Nigel Short to the single victory for which the whole world of chess is now willing him.

1	d4	d5
2	c4	e6

Short continues his policy of switching his openings. The Slav has done its job and he reverts to the Queen's Gambit Declined, one of his most successful openings over the last few years. Naturally Kasparov would have prepared well for it in the months leading up to the game, but then, so would Short, and this is a solid and sound opening.

3	♘c3	♘f6
4	cxd5	

The Exchange Variation is an old favourite of Kasparov's: he has scored some brilliant victories with it and Short must have been expecting it.

4	...	exd5
5	♗g5	♗e7
6	e3	0-0
7	♗d3	♘bd7
8	♘ge2	♖e8

White has a choice between castling on the kingside; or playing 9 ♕c2 and castling queenside – a much riskier alternative.

9 0-0

As Kasparov has proved before, White has good chances to build an attack from this position as well, but he does so from a solid basis.

9	...	♘f8
10	b4	

This pawn cannot be taken: 10...♗xb4? 11 ♗xf6 gxf6 12 ♘xd5! ♕xd5 13 ♕a4, forking bishop and rook.

10	...	a6

11 a3

This gives us a clue to Kasparov's middlegame intentions. White has two plans in this position: to advance his b- and a-pawns to weaken Black's queenside; and to advance in the centre with f3 and e4. If Kasparov had wanted to carry out the first mentioned idea, then he would have played 11 ♖b1 and 12 a4.

11	...	c6
12	♕c2	g6
13	f3	

Mikhail Botvinnik, former world champion and Kasparov's early mentor, was one of the first to employ this plan of advancing in the centre with e4.

13 ...   ♘e6
14 ♗h4

Kasparov revealed that he had already played exactly this position against one of his seconds, Alexander Belyavsky, in a rapid tournament a few years ago. That game bears a frightening similarity to this, and leads one to question exactly what Short had been looking at in his opening preparation.

Belyavsky played 14...♘g7 here, eventually getting stormed on the kingside; Kasparov even employed some similar manoeuvres to this game, including the star move 21 ♘f4.

14 ...   ♘h5
15 ♗xe7   ♖xe7
16 ♕d2

Subtle. Once White plays e4, the queen will look down on the weakened dark squares around Black's king.

16 ...   b6

Kasparov criticised this move afterwards. As he proved in the game, this pawn is a permanent weakness; if there were still a pawn on a7 it would be a different matter, but in this case it is always vulnerable to an attack by White's knight coming to a4.

17 ♖ad1   ♗b7
18 ♗b1   ♘hg7

19 e4

Eventually Kasparov will be looking to push this pawn to e5, and then begin a pawn storm with f3-f4-f5 as in the above mentioned game against Belyavsky. But for the time being there is no rush. Black usually cannot afford to capture on e4 anyway, as it would open the f-file.

19 ...   ♖c8
20 ♗a2   ♖d7
21 ♘f4

This unlikely move is the best of the game. Normally, if your opponent is cramped, the last thing you want to do is exchange pieces and relieve the pressure, but Kasparov realises that Black's knights are very good defensive pieces, so he exchanges one of them off. At the time we were sceptical about this move, but the course of the game proves that Kasparov's judgement is simply on a higher plane to the rest of human-kind.

21 ...   ♘xf4

An illustration of the problems

that Black experiences with the weakened pawn on b6 is shown in the variation: 21...♕g5? 22 ♘xe6 ♕xd2 23 ♖xd2 ♘xe6 24 ♘a4! winning material.

22 ♕xf4

The exchange also allows White's queen to penetrate into Black's camp along the dark squares.

22	...	♘e6
23	♕e5	♖e7
24	♕g3	♕c7
25	♕h4	♘g7
26	♖c1	♕d8
27	♖fd1	♖cc7
28	♘a4	

28 ...   dxe4

Short only spent a couple of minutes deciding on this disastrous capture. Encouraged by Kasparov's shortage of time (he only had just over five minutes to make it to move forty), he was looking for a way to complicate the position, rather than sit and do nothing while the world champion quietly improved his position.

28...♖cd7 was better, but then it was Kasparov's intention to play 29 e5, play the bishop back to b1, and then push the f-pawn. No fun at all for Black.

29 fxe4   ♕e8

This is the big idea. The e-pawn is attacked, and if 30 ♖e1 c5! opens the line from Black's queen to the knight on a4. There is, however, a pathetically simple defence.

30 ♘c3

Kasparov played this instantly. White's pawns dominate the centre; he has the open f-file to attack down, supported by the bishop on a2; and there is the threat of e5, followed by ♘e4 to f6, hanging over Black's head.

Although he was running short of time, Kasparov wrapped up the rest of the game with panache.

30	...	♖cd7
31	♕f2	♘e6
32	e5	c5

A desperate attempt to complicate which gets the treatment it deserves, though there was nothing better.

33	bxc5	bxc5
34	d5	♘d4
35	♘e4 *(D)*	

Game over.

35	...	♕d8
36	♘f6+	♔g7
37	♘xd7	♖xd7
38	♖xc5	♘e6
39	♖cc1	

And **Black resigned**.

A brilliant game by Kasparov, and as he described it afterwards,

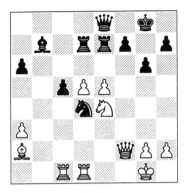

his 'cleanest' of the match so far, though he added: 'I don't have great creative satisfaction from this game ... I analysed this kind of position years ago and I have won many nice games with it.'

All of which begs the question, what exactly had Short been looking at in his pre-match preparations? The Queens Gambit Declined is a sound opening for Black, there is no problem with the choice, but where was the new idea to catch Kasparov off his guard, to make him solve new problems? Playing over this game again, the world champion looked like he was on auto-pilot.

The score: 10½-4½ in Kasparov's favour.

Game 16

Short-Kasparov
Sicilian Najdorf

Rea Short had been keeping a bottle of champagne on ice ever since her husband's challenge began on 7 September. It was finally uncorked on the night of Tuesday, 12 October, to mark his first win. What gave it a special flavour was not just the delay of five weeks, but the gap of seven years since he had last taken a tournament game off the champion.

The audience in the Savoy Theatre erupted in warm applause which gave way to cheering. It was a big moment in British chess, all the more satisfying in that the game had shown every sign of becoming the most boring of the match. Earlier, in the Grandmasters' room, the general prediction had been a draw. Speelman had moved the pieces around and declared that it seemed to be going nowhere. Martin Amis, the novelist and a keen chess follower, had appeared for the first time in the match – then left because it seemed to be a drag.

A key moment came with a possible exchange of queens, a negative ploy which the two players circled around warily, almost daring each other to do it, then backed away. Suddenly, after an innocent-looking knight manoeuvre on the queen's side, Short seemed to have a serious chance. There was general disbelief among the grandmasters that Kasparov's defences should finally collapse so quickly after so many escapes. It was like the fall of the Berlin Wall.

Then, when Short had the obvious check at his finger-tips, he seemed to hesitate. It was an awful moment for the lookers-on. His hand wavered for a moment in the air over the piece as the experts shrieked backstage, 'Go on, it's a killer.' Keene was beside himself in the commentary box. Then the hand moved and the deed was done. Kasparov muttered something, then quit the stage abruptly. It was his first defeat at the chessboard by anyone for a year. It was a new experience for the champion to slink away to an inquest with his advisers, leaving the Englishman alone under the spotlights with the media to relish his first moment of glory in the match.

What cheered Short's supporters was not just the fact of the win, but the assured manner in which it was achieved. He was held to have outplayed the champion from a broadly equal position with a blazing final attack. Nigel was brutally honest about himself, though, when he admitted that he hadn't realised he was winning until near the end, when 'it was too late to throw it away'.

The sense of joy and relief was reflected all over the challenger's face. He waved triumphantly to the crowd like a boxer. He said afterwards that when he watched the replay of the historic last moments of the game on video he couldn't help jumping up and down shouting 'Go on, you can do it', even though he knew he had won.

Apart from laying a ghost and regaining some self-respect, Short did the bookies a favour, saving William Hill the £10,000 they would have had to pay out if he had failed to win a single game. The odds on him winning the match were halved to 500-1. 'We were very happy to see him win,' said Graham Sharpe, of Hill's. 'We now expect the result will revitalise interest and a lot of money will be going on the next couple of games.'

Short said disarmingly that he could hardly sign the scoresheet since his hand was trembling so much. 'I had almost forgotten what it was like to beat Kasparov. It took him 32 games to win his first one at world level and I did it twice as quickly.' Kasparov's final comment on the game was: 'I made the British public happy, but not myself.' What annoyed him was not so much losing a game, which was bound to happen at some time, but what he described as the 'stupid' play that allowed it to happen.

Short had avoided the first 'whitewash' in a world championship since the one inflicted on Emanuel Lasker by the Cuban, José Raoul Capablanca, in 1921. Lasker in his turn had whitewashed three challengers, Marshall, Janowsky and Tarrasch – the same Dr Siegbert Tarrasch who had once written: 'Chess, like love, like music, has the power to make men happy.' Nigel Short may have come to doubt that theory in the course of this match, but not tonight.

1	e4	c5
2	♘f3	d6
3	d4	cxd4
4	♘xd4	♘f6
5	♘c3	a6
6	♗c4	e6
7	♗b3	b5

Kasparov varies from 7...♘bd7 which he played in games 6,8 and 10; and from 7...♘c6 in games 12 and 14.

Pushing the b-pawn down the board is classic Najdorf strategy: if the knight on c3 can be pushed away, then the e4 pawn will be vulnerable. When Bobby Fischer first began playing this variation for White, he used to throw his f-pawn down the board to f5 to try to break open the diagonal for the bishop on b3. Antidotes were eventually found for Black, and the modern way of playing the position is to try and attack using the pieces, rather than pawns.

    8 0-0   ♗e7
    9 ♕f3

This threatens e5, attacking the rook on a8 and knight on f6.

    9 ...   ♕c7

If now 10 e5 dxe5 11 ♕xa8 exd4 the complications favour Black.

    10 ♕g3

The queen takes up a strong attacking position, bearing down on g7.

    10 ...   ♘c6

Exchanging off White's aggressively placed knight before it does any damage.

    11 ♘xc6   ♕xc6

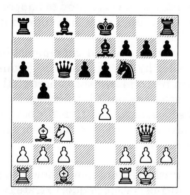

For the next three moves Kasparov leaves the g-pawn so that it can be taken, but don't imagine that he does this lightly. In each case he would gain persistent pressure down the g-file. On this turn, for instance, it would simply be a mistake for White to grab it: 12 ♕xg7 ♖g8 13 ♕h6 ♘xe4 14

♘xe4 ♕xe4, and Black has regained the pawn and has an attack to boot.

    12 ♖e1   ♗b7
    13 a3   ♖d8

This looks odd but is in fact a subtle plan that defuses White's attacking potential. Short must waste a move before going on the attack as Kasparov has not yet committed his king, and the best he can come up with is ...

    14 f3

A solid move, but now it will be impossible to reinforce an attack by swinging the rooks over to the kingside on the third rank. Now Kasparov may safely castle. If instead 14 ♕xg7? ♖g8 15 ♕h6 d5! 16 exd5? ♘xd5 17 ♘xd5 ♖xd5! with a decisive attack on g2.

    14 ...   0-0
    15 ♗h6   ♘e8

This is only a temporary inconvenience for Black – the bishop must soon retreat.

    16 ♔h1   ♔h8
    17 ♗g5   ♗xg5
    18 ♕xg5   ♘f6

The opening has been a success for Kasparov. He has developed his pieces harmoniously, prevented Short from mounting an attack, and has a solid, compact pawn structure. Kasparov had used under half an hour to get to this position, an indication that it was all home analysis; anyway, this kind of position has been seen quite a few times before from this opening.

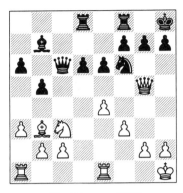

19 ♖ad1   ♖d7
20 ♖d3

Short can think of nothing better to do than double rooks on the d-file, bearing down on Black's only weakness, the pawn on d6, though as Kasparov's next move emphatically shows, there is little likelihood of the pawn ever being won.

20 ...   ♖fd8
21 ♖ed1   ♕c5
22 ♕e3

If White exchanges on c5 then he would stand worse in the ending as Black's queenside pawns could constitute a threat.

22 ...   ♔g8

An ending is on the cards, so it seems sensible to move the king towards the centre of the board. At this point a draw was being universally predicted. Afterwards even Short admitted that the game was looking like the most boring of the match, and that he was just shuffling his pieces round, too lazy to offer a draw. It's a good job he didn't.

23 ♔g1   ♔f8
24 ♕f2   ♗a8

Most of us found that one baffling, but it hardly changes the position very much. Perhaps making a 'pass' move was Kasparov's way of offering a draw, without being seen to 'beg' for one. It's a matter of pride. The onus is really on Short to make the offer as he is playing with the White pieces.

25 ♘e2   g6?

It is extraordinary how a game can turn on just one move. There seems to be nothing in particular going on in the position, and perhaps half expecting Short to offer a draw, Kasparov drops his guard for one fatal moment. I would guess that Kasparov had intended to meet 26 ♘d4 with 26...e5, only to discover that 27 ♖c3! ♕a7 (or 27...♕b6 28 ♘e6+!) 28 ♘c6 ♕xf2+ 29 ♔xf2 ♖c8 30 ♘xe5! wins material. Of course Black can bail out into an ending with 29...♗xc6 30 ♖xc6, but considering 30...a5 31 ♖b6, he must lose a pawn. Instead of 25...g6, 25...♕xf2+ 26 ♔xf2 ♔e7 is completely equal.

26 ♘d4!

Black can no longer exchange queens, so his king appears misplaced on f8, and 25...g6 looks ugly and weakening. White's immediate threat is 27 ♗xe6 fxe6 28 ♘xe6+, and the natural move to prevent this, 26...♔g8, runs into 27 ♘xe6! ♕xf2+ 28 ♔xf2 fxe6 29 ♗xe6+ ♔g7 30 ♗xd7 ♖xd7 31 ♖xd6, destroying Black's position.

26 ...   ♛e5
Optically this looks fine, but Short proves that the queen is vulnerable in the centre of the board.

27 ♖e1
Threatening 28 f4, and inducing Kasparov to weaken his king position further.

27 ...   g5
Short plays superbly during the next phase of the game, manoeuvring patiently on the queenside, not ruffled by Kasparov's build up on the kingside which, as he correctly judged, should not be at all dangerous.

28 c3   ♚g7
29 ♝c2   ♖g8
30 ♘b3   ♚f8
31 ♖d4   ♚e7
32 a4!
Making the b-pawn a target.

32 ...   h5
33 axb5   axb5
34 ♖b4
Short's approach, continuing his assault on the b-pawn, is consistent and strong.

34 ...   h4 *(D)*
'Black's position is so yucky, all he can do is charge ahead and hope for the best.' – American grandmaster Joel Benjamin writing in the official match bulletin.

35 ♘d4   g4
36 ♖xb5
Short has nibbled around the edges of Kasparov's position, and is finally getting stuck into the middle. The queen has no decent square. If 36...♛f4 37 ♛xh4; and

36...♛xh2+ 37 ♚xh2 g3+ 38 ♚g1 gxf2+ 39 ♚xf2 leaves White a pawn up for nothing.

36 ...   d5
37 ♛xh4
Nice and simple. 37 ♘f5+ also wins, e.g. 37...exf5 38 exf5 ♘e4 39 ♖xe4, or 37...♚e8 38 exd5.

37 ...   ♛h5
38 ♘f5+
And **Kasparov resigned**.

A clean kill. If 38...exf5 39 exf5+ ♚f8 40 ♛xf6, and Black's defences are destroyed.

A well played game. Kasparov's opening preparation was clearly superior and he equalised the position with little difficulty; but Short held his nerve, played sensibly, and one error from the world champion was enough for him to take control and force a win in convincing style.

Afterwards, Short looked relieved and delighted. He knew the match was beyond salvation, but he had regained some honour and self-respect.

The score: 10½-5½ to Kasparov.

Game 17
Kasparov-Short
Scotch Opening

Remarkably, in the last eight games Short's score has been level with Kasparov's. Could he finally go one better and win a second game, as the bookies had predicted? It would be a splendid final flourish, proving to the sceptics that, far from suffering the psychological collapse many had feared after his catastrophic start, he had come back fighting and even gaining in mental strength.

The win had certainly done wonders for his self-confidence. He told Daniel Johnson that he now believed 'for the first time' that he was capable of wresting the world championship away from Kasparov, though he had to admit that his chances of doing so on this occasion were as slim as those of England reaching the finals of football's World Cup. England lost 2-0 to Holland, in fact, the very next day, putting them virtually out of contention.

'I feel it was a pity to win *this* game, though, not games eight or ten, when I felt I played better,' he added. 'I've deserved to win several games earlier, and I think I can do it again.' He said Kasparov had been 'bloody fortunate' to avoid losing before.

He would not allow the champion to blame his errors in the sixteenth game on the fact that he had been 'tired and emotionally exhausted'. 'He can't tolerate the fact that I have been playing on equal terms with him,' he said. 'He's used to me collapsing, as I used to do before this match. Now something has happened. So he thinks it has to be something wrong with him, because it can't be something *right* with me. He likes to think that if only he didn't have these worries – personal, political, whatever – he would win every game. It's not modesty at all – it's the reverse.

'I feel very much at ease. Maybe for the first time I've started to imagine that I could become world champion. My chances of winning this match are minute, but that won't stop me trying. Next time I play him in a long match, though, things will be different.'

The British victory had lifted the cloud hanging over the match and altered the tone in which it was covered in the press. It was no longer a national embarrassment just to mention it. Short was no longer talked about like Graham Taylor, the England manager, who had been branded a 'turnip' by the *Sun*. The popular papers started talking about family chess and encouraging people to play it.

In the *Telegraph* Michael Green recalled Action Chess in the Thirties, Forties and Fifties, which could be played anywhere – in tuckshops at school, army canteens, YMCAs and railway waiting-rooms. He recalled using a pepper pot, a coffee spoon and even a prawn from his salad as makeshift pieces on a square-patterned tablecloth (the poisoned prawn?).

'Men played in bombers over Germany. Soldiers carried a set in their battledress. I actually achieved one brief game in a tank. I played Action Chess in hospital, calling out the moves to a man across the ward. I shall never forget the triumph in his voice as he cried out one evening, "Rook takes queen, check, and get out of that, you bastard." When I woke up in the morning, his bed was empty. He had died in the night. But he was right. It was checkmate.'

There was no checkmate, however – and no sudden death – in the 17th game, which was inevitably an anti-climax after Short's much-heralded win. But the challenger played well to block Kasparov's attempted march to victory with White. The match score was now 11-6. Despite Short's belated recovery, the champion needed only one more point to retain his title. Kasparov was closing for the kill.

1	e4	e5
2	♘f3	♘c6
3	d4	exd4
4	♘xd4	♗c5
5	♘xc6	

The match is beginning to look like a series of training games more than a world championship final. Against all predictions, the players are repeating the same arcane variation of the Scotch as game 11.

5	...	♕f6
6	♕d2	dxc6
7	♘c3	♗e6
8	♘a4	♖d8
9	♗d3	♗d4
10	0-0	a6

Short's improvement on game 11, where he played 10...♘e7 and quickly stood worse. 10...a6 is a sensible move. If the bishop on d4 is attacked by the pawn moving to c3, then it can always drop back to the a7 square.

11 ♘c3

'Hardly the manoeuvre of the year,' commented England's number 2, Michael Adams, over in the Grandmasters' analysis room, but this calm retreat began to win the pundits round – particularly as the alternatives were even worse. In the TV studio, Jonathan Speelman confessed to me – off air, I should add – that their team had missed this retreat, and that he was impressed by it. Once more the Russians proved better prepared.

11 ... ♘e7

12 ♘e2 ♗b6

It is best to drop the bishop back here rather than a7, to keep the c7 pawn covered. 12...♗xb2 fails to 13 ♗xb2 ♕xb2 14 ♖ab1 ♕xa2 15 ♕c3, threatening both g7 and 16 ♖a1 winning the queen.

13 ♕f4

The one thing that White has going for him in this position is his better pawn structure. By exchanging queens he hopes to negate the effect of Black's active pieces, and looks forward to pushing his sound majority of pawns on the kingside.

13 ... ♘g6

As in game 13, Short accepts a damaged pawn structure, but hopes that the activity of his pieces will compensate for it, a discussion which Kasparov is eager to revive. Afterwards the world champion was dismissive of Short's idea, maintaining that

it was simply incorrect, while Nigel was rather proud of it: he was breaking the rules again and, once more, he gets away with it. Instead of the principled queen exchange, Kasparov could also have played 14 ♕g3, threatening 15 ♗g5, an idea which is just as promising as the game continuation. It is more a matter of taste than anything else.

14 ♕xf6 gxf6

15 ♘g3 h5

16 ♗e2 h4

The h-pawn gives Black good counterplay.

17 ♘f5 ♗xf5

18 exf5

White has traded one long-term advantage for another: his pawn structure is also damaged, but he now has the bishop pair.

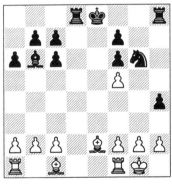

18 ... ♘e5

19 ♖e1 ♔f8

20 ♗f4

20 a4 was strongly advocated – by Michael Adams in particular – but Kasparov said afterwards that

he had rejected it on account of
20...a5 21 ♖a3!? ♖d4, when White
is tied to the defence of the a-
pawn

| 20 ... | ♖d4 |
| 21 g3 | ♔g7 |

An inaccuracy. It was better to
play 21...hxg3, when White is
forced to recapture with the h-
pawn (22 ♗xg3 ♖d2 with pressure; or 22 fxg3 ♖xf4+). After 22
hxg3, White can no longer create
a passed pawn on the kingside
(compare with the game).

22 ♖ad1	♖e4
23 ♔g2	hxg3
24 fxg3?	

The strange thing about this
blunder is that Kasparov had
seen that 24 hxg3 was a mistake
because of 24...♗xf2, but had failed
to realise that 24...♗f2 would still
be strong even if it wasn't capturing a pawn.

Opinion was divided on how
large White's advantage would be
after 24 ♗xg3. When analysing
this position with us in the TV
studio after the game, Kasparov
suggested the line 24...♖he8 25
♗f3!? ♖xe1 26 ♖xe1 ♖d8 27 ♖d1,
saying, 'This is my dream after
the opening, Black should be struggling to draw,' a reference to his
superior pawn structure, which
has given him a passed pawn on
the kingside. Short was cooler
about White's prospects, but he
did not dispute that the advantage would have been with Kasparov.

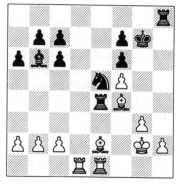

| 24 ... | ♗f2! |

I have never seen Kasparov
look so unsettled by a move. He
shook his head violently as if trying to wake from sleep, unable to
believe what he had just done,
and muttered angrily to himself
in utter disgust.

As it is, luck is on his side. He
loses a pawn, but that is all, and
in view of Black's damaged structure, it is not enough to win the
game.

25 ♔xf2	♖xh2+
26 ♔f1	♖exe2
27 ♖xe2	♖h1+
28 ♔f2	♖xd1
29 b3	

A lesser player than Kasparov
might have been thrown by missing a shot like 24...♗f2, but to his
great credit, he readjusts to his
new task of playing for a draw
rather than a win with great
speed. It was possible to play 29
♗xe5 fxe5 30 ♖xe5, but after
30...♔f6, White must still work
to draw. It is much safer to keep
the bishop, which in this case is a

clearly superior piece to the knight.

29 ...   Ëd7

In order to defend the c7 pawn.

30 Ëd2!

Exchanging rooks is the surest way to draw.

30 ...   Ëxd2+

31 Âxd2   c5

Desperately trying to make something of his queenside pawn majority, but with the king stuck way over on the kingside it is all in vain.

32 ±e3   c6

33 ±e4   c4

34 b4   b5

35 Âf4   Ìd7

36 ±d4

The knight cannot move from d7, or White's king penetrates through to the queenside pawns.

With such a restriction, Black is unable to play for a win.

36 ...   ±f8

37 Âc7

Preventing Black's king from moving over to the queenside.

37 ...   ±e7

38 g4   ±f8

39 Âd6+   ±g7

40 Âc7   ±f8

41 a3

Having satisfied himself that there was no possibility of making further progress, Short offered a **draw**, which Kasparov accepted immediately.

Kasparov's claims that he stood better in the endgame sound more like the protestations of a man who can't accept that he has been caught out by such an unorthodox idea, rather any objective truth seeker. Naturally, Short disagreed with him, saying that he liked his doubled pawns, and that chances were 'balanced'.

In a sense it is rather a pointless argument. The course of the game demonstrated that the position was sufficiently murky for White not to get a grip on it, and in the complications Kasparov lost his way. Another good performance from Short.

The score: 11-6 to Kasparov.

Game 18

Short-Kasparov
Sicilian Najdorf

In their pre-match forecasts, most British grandmasters had estimated that the match would be concluded – in Kasparov's favour, naturally – by games 18, 19 or 20. It was beginning to look as though they would be proved right, which left open the question of what should happen in the remaining games.

The 24-game format had been set originally for the needs of Predict-a-Move, which had been a flop, as part of a sponsorship deal which was now inoperative, so in theory it could still be changed if both players agreed. At this stage, however, Short was still insisting on the full 24 games, even though they would be played out as an undramatic anti-climax, with 'all passion spent'. The experience of playing more games with Kasparov would doubtless assist his long-term chess education.

For his part, Kasparov had long ago regarded the whole match as an extended training session, which had now gone on long enough. He wanted to change the format into something more entertaining for the players and public alike. Until game 9, he had played the match as a normal world championship bout, with total concentration, aiming to score points and win. Since then, however, when he knew that with five wins his title was in the bag, he and his seconds had been engaged in higher chess analysis, sometimes taking Short's openings and playing them back to him with new developments and variations.

When he had talked about being tired, he had meant it. The exhaustion was not just a result of the chess, though the three-days-a-week format was unrelenting. He had many other matters on his mind. The situation in Russia occupied more and more of his waking thoughts. Although he never doubted that Yeltsin would succeed in seeing off what he regarded as the remnants of the Soviet Communist system, he found his attention straying constantly to the news coverage on CNN to learn the latest developments.

He was also involved in the detail of the new Professional Chess Association, the breakaway organisation set up by Short and himself to stage the world championship. To give itself credibility outside FIDE, the PCA had to show the world's leading players that it was capable of organising its own tournaments and raising its own sponsorship. In order to defy FIDE, the grandmasters needed reassurance that the PCA was really a going concern, and not just a vehicle to enrich Kasparov and Short.

They were pressing for firm information about the first PCA tournament, due at Groningen in Holland in December. Kasparov might be playing a world championship match, the highest pinnacle in chess, but these people needed an answer, and in the absence of a secretariat to service the new organisation most of the PCA's work fell to the champion and his manager, Andrew Page. There was also a speed chess tour round the world to be sponsored and planned for 1994.

In addition to that, Kasparov and Page had a business to run. Their Muscovy Trading Company had set up an air charter firm in Russia which had just clinched its first contract. Page had to take time off from the match to go to Moscow to handle it. He was there during the White House crisis and was surprised to see how little it had affected the lives of ordinary Russians, who went about their business as if nothing remarkable had happened.

It was business as usual, too, in the Savoy Theatre, as Kasparov pressed for the win that would retain his world title. Short was playing White, which made a final denouement less likely. The experts gave Short a slight advantage as he massed for attack, but Kasparov, as Keene put it, 'erected a Maginot line of defensive fortifications' in front of the black king that eventually frustrated him. Afterwards Short denied that he had been reluctant to take risks for fear of losing both the game and the match. 'I am prepared to take risks to win in the remaining games – if they are justified. I feel rather good and I'm starting to play rather well.'

Kasparov said: 'There was a lot of underneath tension in this game. Maybe I can now finish the title in just one game.' Short chipped in: 'I have a different opinion.'

1	e4	c5
2	♘f3	d6
3	d4	cxd4
4	♘xd4	♘f6
5	♘c3	a6
6	♗c4	e6
7	♗b3	b5
8	0-0	♗e7
9	♕f3	♕c7
10	♕g3	0-0

The first deviation from game 16, in which Kasparov played 10...♘c6. He is employing some subtle psychology. Earlier in the year he had played exactly this position as White against Boris Gelfand, at the elite grandmaster tournament in Linares, Spain, winning a beautiful game. It is almost as though he is playing against himself.

11	♗h6	♘e8
12	♖ad1	♗d7
13	♘f3	

Short is following Kasparov's own recipe. Here Gelfand tried 13...b4, but got clobbered after 14 ♘e2 a5 15 ♘f4, and Kasparov soon crashed through on e6. Kasparov plays the move recommended by Gelfand after the game.

| 13 ... | a5 |
| 14 a4 | |

Also recommended by Gelfand, who assessed this position as being slightly better for White. Kasparov wants it proved. It was ominous that he was bashing out his moves, while Nigel was using up a good deal of time.

| 14 ... | b4 |
| 15 ♘e2 | ♘c6 |

We were examining the blunt plan of 15...♘a6, intending ...♘c5 hitting e4, b3 and a4. However,

this looks way too slow if White lunges straight away with 16 e5, followed by swinging the rook into the attack via d4.

| 16 ♘f4 | ♗f6 |

Short now has some highly tempting attacking continuations at his disposal, which, for the sake of prudence, he chose to ignore. I think his judgement was correct, particularly as it was evident that Kasparov was still in his home analysis.

The most obvious try is 17 ♘h5, but the audacious 17...♗xb2! is fine in view of 18 e5 ♘xe5 19 ♗xg7 ♘xf3+ and 20...♗xg7.

| 17 ♘d3 | |

Defending the b2 pawn.

| 17 ... | e5 |

This closes the position down. White's knight on d3 cannot return to the kingside, and the possibility for White to break with e5 is also ruled out. On the negative side, it does weaken the d5 square and open the diagonal for the bishop on b3, though this can be countered by playing the bishop to e6.

| 18 ♗e3 | |

Covering d4 in readiness for ♘d2.

| 18 ... | ♗e7! |

A strong re-grouping. Black's knight returns to its natural square on f6.

| 19 ♘d2 | ♘f6 |

I felt that White ought to have the better chances here, but it is certainly very difficult to prove.

The approach Short selects in the game is too slow, so perhaps 20 f4!? is indicated. Kasparov stated that it was his intention to meet that with 20...♘g4, and then how about 21 ♘c4!?. The situation is extremely complicated, and impossible to evaluate.

If Nigel had had more energy, he might have tried something like this, but his play in this game shows signs of extreme tiredness.

20	f3	♖fe8
21	♔h1	♗e6
22	♖fe1	♖ac8
23	♕f2	

The shuffling is done, and now it is time for action.

| 23 | ... | d5! |
| 24 | ♗b6 | |

Simply 24 exd5 was more sensible than this. Kasparov now gets the better game.

24	...	♕b8
25	♗c5	♗xc5
26	♘xc5	♘d4!
27	♘xe6	fxe6
28	exd5	♘xb3

28...exd5 was more ambitious, but he was anxious that after 29 ♘e4 ♘xb3 30 ♘xf6+ gxf6 31 cxb3 his king would be slightly exposed. However, if he had really wanted to win then this is what he would have tried: the potential strength of Black's d-pawn outweighs any problems he might have with his king.

29	♘xb3	exd5
30	♘xa5	♕a8
31	♘b3	♕xa4
32	♖a1	♕c6
33	♖e2	

Kasparov has the better position because of his pawn centre and pressure on the c2 pawn, but it is very difficult to make anything of it. After thinking for a quarter of an hour he played ...

| 33 | ... | d4 |

... and offered a **draw**, which was accepted by Short after little reflection. He actually has a forced line at his disposal: 34 ♖ae1 ♘d5 (threatening ...♘e3) 35 ♖xe5 ♖xe5 36 ♖xe5 ♕xc2 37 ♕xc2 ♖xc2 38 ♖xd5 ♖xb2 39 h4 ♖xb3 40 ♖xd4, with a technical draw.

A disappointing game. A complicated middlegame was reached, but neither player was prepared to take any great risk in playing for a win, so a draw was the inevitable result. Kasparov is happy to inch closer to the magic 12½ points, while Short does not wish to lose another game.

The score: 11½-6½ in favour of Kasparov

Game 19

Kasparov-Short
Ruy Lopez, Steinitz Variation Deferred

In the event, Short could not prevent Kasparov from acquiring the half-point he needed to retain the title, but he ensured that the champion would have to wait at least two more days before he could pocket the winner's £1 million cheque.

As the players shook hands on stage after agreeing the 26-move draw, the audience applauded, many of them thinking Kasparov must have won the game. Even the commentators were assuming that. The position on the board was so confused, in fact, that nobody could tell who held the advantage, as the contestants themselves concluded after a lengthy post-mortem. Short finally exclaimed: 'Let's face it, we don't have a clue what's happening.'

With the benefit of overnight analysis, Kasparov confirmed that a draw had been the correct outcome, even though he was a pawn up playing White. He had felt he was losing control of the position and wanted to play safe. Offering a draw at that point was a good option for him, because Short would either accept – in which case Kasparov secured the half-point he needed to retain his title – or he would use up valuable time on the clock thinking about it. Either way Kasparov had nothing to lose.

Short accepted the draw reluctantly, because it brought an end to his dream of capturing the world title. The champion admitted that Short was playing better than he had at the beginning. 'At the same time,' he added, 'I don't think that the problems he is facing are equal to the problems I managed to bring to the table in the first nine games.'

Short told Daniel Johnson after this game: 'Kasparov is still a fantastic player, a worthy world champion. But I have exposed weaknesses in his game ... If we were to start again now, my chances would be very much better.' It was true that he had stayed level with Kasparov in the second half of the match, but this was only after the result had been effectively settled. Had he stayed level with Kasparov over the first 12 games instead, that would have been a very different story, setting up a real sporting contest.

For all the artificial drama built up by *The Times* – 'Short Goes Down Fighting' and so on – it was in truth a bit of an anti-climax. The *Daily*

Mail said the match had 'failed to capture the nation's imagination. People resolutely stayed away ... Even a visit by the Princess of Wales, and saturation TV coverage, did little to enliven the battle.'

The *Guardian* was equally bleak, saying Short's challenge had been 'scarred by failure on the board and off-stage recriminations'. His relations with fellow British grandmasters had been soured, audiences had dwindled, the Predict-a-Move competition had been cancelled through lack of interest, and *The Times*, it reported with some satisfaction, 'is thought to have lost at least £2 million on the venture.'

Peter McKay, of the London *Evening Standard*, said the problem was 'Nigel's attitude. He says some terribly nerdish things that make you cringe. He is attended by two journalists who – if we didn't know them to be men of substance and great charm – have every appearance of being nerds themselves. I refer to Dominic Lawson, editor of the *Spectator*, and Peter Stothard, editor of *The Times*. The suggestion is that they have increased Nigel's latent nerdishness. I doubt it, though. It seems simply to be his character.'

Cathy Forbes, who wrote Short's biography, rallied to his defence: 'I think the people who are carping are jealous that Nigel is challenging Kasparov and they are not,' she said. 'I can't remember a day in the last week when I've met someone who has not known what was happening in the match. TV will never be able to ignore a major chess event again.'

Meanwhile, even though he was standing on the brink of certain defeat, the challenger maintained his defiant posture. 'The twentieth game,' he declared, 'is important. I'd like to cause Kasparov some damage.'

Garry Kasparov now has 11½ points. He needs a draw to retain his title; and one more win to finish the match and bag the major share of the £1.7 million prize fund. Surely he would go for a win today with the advantage of the white pieces?

1 e4	e5
2 ♘f3	♘c6
3 ♗b5	a6
4 ♗a4	d6

A good choice. Short throws Kasparov off familiar territory by playing the so-called 'Steinitz Variation Deferred' for the first time in his life. The most notable adherents of this system in top-level chess are the Hungarian grandmaster Lajos Portisch, and Jan Timman. It is quite possible that Nigel had recognised the viability of the opening when preparing for Timman, and decided now to put his work to good use.

5 ♗xc6+	bxc6
6 d4	exd4

Black can also maintain the

centre with 6...f6, but Short has had good results with that position from the White side, and prefers to release the central tension instead.

7 ♕xd4   ♘f6

This is slightly unusual. Timman likes to play his knight to e7 to avoid the danger of White pushing on in the centre with e5.

8 0-0   ♗e7
9 e5

A well-motivated move, breaking up Black's cluster of pawns.

9 ...   c5
10 ♕d3   dxe5
11 ♕xd8+   ♗xd8
12 ♘xe5

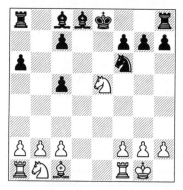

The discussion continues. Kasparov believes he stands better because of Black's split pawns on the queenside; whilst Short believes that his possession of the bishop pair and active pieces fully compensate.

12 ...   ♗e7
13 ♖e1

According to my sources, the first new move of the game. Van der Wiel-Portisch, Holland 1990, continued instead 13 ♘c3 ♗f5 14 ♖e1 0-0 15 ♘c6 ♗d6 16 ♘e7+ ♗xe7 17 ♖xe7 ♖fe8, and the game was agreed drawn. Thrilling.

13 ...   0-0
14 ♗g5   ♗e6
15 ♘d2

It is essential for White to develop all his pieces before taking any action. For instance, 15 ♘d7!? ♘xd7! 16 ♗xe7 ♖fe8 17 ♗g5 ♗xa2! winning a pawn because of the back-rank trick.

15 ...   ♖fe8
16 h3   h6
17 ♗h4   ♖ad8
18 ♘df3   g5
19 ♗g3   ♗d5
20 ♖ad1   ♔g7

This rather puzzled those of us watching. It can be useful to take the king off the back rank, but wasn't there something more active? For instance, if Black wishes to take the policy of wrecking his pawn structure to an extreme then 20...♘h5 21 ♗h2 ♘f4 22 ♗xf4 gxf4 should be examined. It is not immediately apparent how to take advantage of Black's ruinous pawns. I wish Nigel had played this, if only to wind Gazza up.

21 c4   ♗b7
22 ♖xd8

It began to dawn on us that the position was not looking at all rosy for Black. We rejected 22...♖xd8 23 ♘c6! fairly quickly, and concentrated on trying to defend the ending after 22...♗xd8 23 ♘d3, though it certainly wasn't a barrel of laughs for Black. With every exchange the weakness of the doubled c-pawns becomes more pronounced.

22 ...	♖xd8

What has Nigel got in mind? The prophets of doom were already predicting an early presentation ceremony.

23	♘c6	♗xc6
24	♖xe7	♖d1+
25	♔h2	♘e4

Kasparov thought for a long time over his next move, which made us reconsider our earlier assessment of 'winning for White': he must have seen that Short could develop some counterplay.

26 ♖xc7

Suddenly the game was over. There was great confusion and some spectators believed that Short had resigned. When it became clear that a **draw** had been agreed, there was consternation. My co-commentator on Channel 4,

Raymond Keene, exclaimed on air, 'Well, I'm buggered!'; and frankly, I was amazed that Short wasn't too.

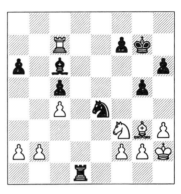

However, the more we looked at the position, the more it seemed that Black's counterplay was sufficient. The problem for Kasparov is that his king is boxed in and cannot easily escape from Black's attack. Take, for instance, some of these variations which Kasparov demonstrated afterwards: 26...♗d7 (this has to be Black's starting move, cutting White's rook out of play) 27 ♖a7 h5 28 ♖xa6 f6! (a cunning move, limiting the freedom of White's pieces before attacking; the threat is ...h4 and ♘xf2, so ...) 29 h4 g4 30 ♘g1 ♘xg3 31 fxg3 ♖d2 32 ♖a7 ♔g6 33 ♘e2 ♖xe2 34 ♖xd7 ♖xb2, with a positional draw.

Or alternatively, instead of 28 ♖xa6 in the above line, 28 ♗e5+ ♔g6 29 ♖xa6+ ♔f5 30 ♗c3 g4 31 hxg4 hxg4, and Black has a screaming attack.

In these lines I find it extraordinary that even when one or two pawns down, Black can build the attack slowly and carefully. The opposite-coloured bishops help Black here, for they make it more difficult for White to exchange off the attacking pieces.

Afterwards the players were asked why they had been content with a draw. Kasparov: 'Because of the match situation I hoped to go for a quiet game today. I don't like taking risks; I respect my opponent. At the end it was extremely complicated – I couldn't evaluate the position.' Short: 'My best chance was in the final position – I don't understand it though, I haven't got a clue what is going on.'

I have a feeling that if either player had had more energy, then they would have played the position on. They were both drained at the end, physically and mentally.

The score: 12-7 to Kasparov who thus retains the title, and now just needs another half point from the next five games to win one million pounds.

Game 20

Short-Kasparov
Sicilian Najdorf

The damage promised by Short after the last game proved not to be fatal, and the match finally reached its predictable end on Thursday, October 21, when the two players agreed on a draw in front of about 200 people, the smallest audience for the whole event. This time it was Short who offered the draw after 36 moves when he found himself with no real winning chances.

That put the score at 12.5 points to 7.5, which is roughly where the experts guessed it would be at the start. The last world rankings of the two players, before FIDE deprived them of their official status, were 2805 for Kasparov, the highest figure ever recorded, and 2665 for Short. A statistical projection based on that gap of 140 points would give Kasparov victory by a slightly higher margin than the one he achieved. It is possible, therefore, to argue that Short's performance was something like one point ahead of expectations.

That would have been fine if those expectations had not been raised to unrealistic levels by the tireless 'hype' generated by *The Times*. The effect was to make the scale of Short's subsequent defeat more disappointing than it needed to be. Their heroic inflation of the challenger's chances – linking him with 'the other Nigel', Nigel Mansell, the motor racing wizard, for example, and describing his defeats as moral victories – did neither him nor the match any favours.

Wallace Arnold, satirical columnist in the *Independent on Sunday*, put this point across beautifully: 'Nigel has, by any stretch of the imagination, played quite remarkably well – brilliantly even – against the dread Russian Kasparov, who is now visibly wilting under the pressure. In every single game they have played, Kasparov has been outclassed time and again by the sheer temerity and intellectual stamina of the Battling Briton. Yet the supercilious critics will simply not acknowledge the fact, preferring to play the simple "numbers game" and to point to the final scores, so as to suggest that Kasparov is ostensibly "winning".

'From the point of view of the audience in the Savoy Theatre – often well into double figures, incidentally – there is no question as to who is the rightful victor. For sheer bravura and good sportsmanship, it simply has to be Nigel, with the untrustworthy Russian trailing way behind.'

There was one blessing, though. The players finally agreed to call a halt to the match when the winning post was reached and not to go through the motions of the final four games that were scheduled. Instead, they settled for a speed chess challenge and, in addition, Kasparov agreed to play at each session against five members of the audience, who would be chosen by the drawing of lots.

There were two unscripted diversions on the final day. Grandmaster Tony Miles, who had been free with his opinions throughout the match, was dismissed from the commentary box for making negative remarks about the sponsor. Having been relegated to delivering his commentaries in one of the Savoy Theatre bars, he repeated the offence and again, as Leonard Barden put it, 'suffered redundancy'. I noted that this particular item of news was not thought worthy of inclusion the next day in *The Times*'s otherwise blanket coverage of the event.

The second diversion was a fire alarm, which turned out to be a malfunction, but nonetheless emptied the theatre very fast, Short leaving the stage before he had time to seal his next move.

The alarm might well have been set off by the heat generated in that morning's *Times* by Daniel Johnson, who, having apparently absorbed some of his father Paul's notorious bile, raged at those commentators, including this one, who had dared to present the match as anything less than a triumph for all concerned, especially Nigel Short and *The Times*.

'Over the past seven weeks,' he wrote, 'a circus gathered around the two central figures: walk-on parts for celebrities like Stephen Fry or Clive Anderson or politicians like Jim Callaghan and Michael Fallon; a whole posse of novelists, including Martin Amis and Julian Barnes; starring opportunities for some of the chess understudies, such as Danny King and Cathy Forbes; cameo roles for character actors like the *Spectator*'s editor, Dominic Lawson, or the *spiritus rector* of the whole event, Raymond Keene.

'In the background was the doleful wail of a chorus of carping commentators: some were chess journalists, such as Leonard Barden, William Hartston and David Spanier; others were cynical old hacks like Donald Trelford and Peter McKay ... and others who missed no opportunity to tell readers at inordinate length that the match was a bore.'

I won't respond to Mr Johnson's impertinence, except to say that I don't mind in the least being bracketed with the likes of Messrs Barden, Hartston and Spanier. In fact, if I were *The Times*, I'd be worried that such a sage and experienced group of chess experts, all devoted to the game and among its most distinguished writers, should be so critical of the event and the paper's coverage of it.

So the match ended as it began, with bad temper and recriminations – though not, for once, between the players themselves (or at least not in public). Kasparov reserved his anger for FIDE and his old foe Campomanes, whom he attacked at the post-match reception even as he received the £1,062,500 cheque and a Waterford crystal trophy. As a grandmaster observed, no world championship would be complete without Garry's ritual denunciation of 'Campo'.

Short received his cheque for £637,500, along with the praise of Peter Stothard, editor of *The Times*, who turned to him and said: 'You have been cool under fire. You are a hero in our household and to thousands of young people. Britain is proud of you.' In an editorial the paper claimed: 'It proved to be one of the most attractive events for the media ever sponsored by *The Times*, almost comparable to the conquest of Everest.'

Kasparov was back on top of his own Everest, the Chess Olympus he had first climbed eight years before. Although he looked happy enough the next day, smiling for the cameras in a flat cap in Regent's Park, voices were raised to suggest that he would climb no further and might soon begin the descent that all world chess champions have had to face in the past.

Professor Nathan Divinsky, the Canadian chess historian, said: 'This is the beginning of the end for the Kasparov era. For the first time in his career, he has shown fear at the board. He has played safe in the last six games, taking draws where in the past he would have gone hammer and tongs for a win.' Despite Divinsky's intimations of mortality, however, it was hard to see who or what – apart, perhaps, from the monster Californian computer Deep Blue – could beat him in the foreseeable future. Karpov had overwhelmed Timman in the FIDE sideshow described as a contest 'between a has-been and a never-was'. Nonetheless, the Russian was now a shadow of his former self and surely offered no further threat to Kasparov. The beaten challenger was being likened to Boris Spassky, who had lost to Fischer by the same margin in 1972. The comparison was not all that encouraging for Short, for the Russian was never to regain his world title. 'Failure Leaves Short's Next Move in Doubt' was the *Guardian*'s headline on his prospects. He had fallen out with his fellow grandmasters in Britain. He had received no tournament invitations. He had not been well advised, he had said some silly and regrettable things, and even sillier things were said on his behalf. On the other hand, he had earned a fortune.

And who was to say he didn't deserve it? He had worked for many years at his chess for little reward. And, above all, he was the one who had to go out into the Coliseum three times a week and face the lion. He had comported himself there bravely, if not always wisely, especially in those early games where the match was won and lost.

His opponent admittedly had many in-built advantages denied to the British challenger, not least those many years of subsidised training at the highest level as the last great product of the Soviet chess machine. He was now independently rich enough to sustain those benefits from his own purse. Furthermore, he enjoyed the supreme confidence of having appeared in six world championships and had never been beaten in any of them. He also happened to be the greatest nudger of a chess piece the world has ever seen.

There were rumours flying around before the start of the game that the players were going to agree a quick draw, though in the event, and in spite of their evident tiredness, they bowed out with a good fight.

1	e4	c5
2	♘f3	d6
3	d4	cxd4
4	♘xd4	♘f6
5	♘c3	a6
6	♗c4	e6
7	♗b3	b5
8	0-0	♗e7
9	♕f3	♕c7
10	♕g3	0-0
11	♗h6	♘e8
12	♖ad1	♗d7

All the same as game 18, and this time it is Short who is the first to vary.

13 a3

Ray Keene described this as 'wimpish', but, combined with

Short's 15th move, it strikes me as a sound way to play the position. Instead of attempting to rip Gazza's lungs out, Short will use his lead in development and more harmoniously placed pieces to constrict Black. 13 a3 prevents Black pushing the pawn down to b4, unsettling the knight.

13	...	♘c6
14	♘xc6	♗xc6
15	♗f4!	

15 f4 was on the lips of a great many brutes (mine included), but when I saw Short's move, I preferred his more controlled approach. Black cannot move the knight from e8: 15...♘f6 16 ♗xd6 ♗xd6 17 ♕xd6 ♕xd6 18 ♖xd6 ♗xe4 19 ♖fd1!, with great advantage in the endgame. Therefore Black's forces must remain bottled up for some time.

| 15 | ... | ♕b7 |
| 16 | ♖fe1 | a5 |

While Short was thinking over his next move, the fire alarm went off in the theatre. Play was stopped, and the whole building evacuated with more amusement than panic among the spectators, who could see no evidence of flames licking up from behind the safety curtain. A blown fuse under the stage was later deemed to be responsible. The interlude added to the 'end of term' feel to the day. It must have been very difficult for the players to keep their concentration, and I was half expecting them to agree a draw after the break. As it was, the game staggered on, with Short maintaining his pressure.

| 17 | e5! | dxe5 |
| 18 | ♗xe5 *(D)* | |

This bishop is White's key attacking piece. The persistent pressure on g7 makes it difficult for Black to organise his forces.

18	...	♗f6
19	♖d4	♖d8
20	♖xd8	♗xd8

21	♘e2	a4
22	♗a2	b4
23	axb4	♕xb4
24	♗c3	♕b7
25	♘d4	

Kasparov would very much like to play 25...♗f6 here, trying to exchange off the dark-squared bishops, and thus relieve the pressure on his position, but 26 ♘xc6 ♕xc6 27 ♗b4 traps the rook and wins the exchange.

| 25 | ... | ♘f6 |

Interviewed afterwards, Short said: 'When Garry played ...♘f6 I was optimistic; I was hoping to mate directly, but in fact it was a good defensive move.'

The assessment of 25...♘f6 depends on whether Short can blast his way through to Black's king with 26 ♖xe6 fxe6 27 ♘xe6. There are now two principal variations:

(a) 27...♗d5 28 ♗xd5 ♘xd5 29 ♗xg7, with excellent attacking chances, for instance, 29...♖e8 30 ♗e5+ ♔f7 31 ♘xd8+ ♖xd8 32 ♕g7+ ♔e6 33 ♕xb7 winning;

(b) 27...♕f7 28 ♘xg7! ♕xa2 29 ♘f5+ ♔f7 30 ♕g7+ ♔e6 31 ♘d4+ ♔d5, and now, considering that White must take time out to defend against the threat of the back-rank mate with 32 h3, then I imagine that Black can defend, though I wouldn't like to bet a lunch on this one, either way.

Somehow it was predictable that Short wasn't going to chance it, though. He didn't want to risk the shame of finishing with a loss, and was only playing for a win so long as Kasparov had no chances at all.

26 ♘xc6   ♕xc6

White has the nominal advantage of the two bishops, but while the one on a2 bites on the e6 pawn, this counts for little. Short tries his best but it is all to no avail.

27	♖d1	♗e7
28	h3	♖a8
29	♖d4	♘e8!
30	♕d3	♗f6!

Kasparov has re-grouped neatly, and is finally in a position to exchange off the bishop on c3, which is not only a powerful attacking piece, but protects the pawn on b2 as well.

31	♖c4	♕a6
32	♗xf6	♘xf6
33	♕d2	h6
34	♖d4	♕b6
35	c3	a3

The last chance for Short to go for a win is by 36 b4, but leaving a pawn on a3 was not to his taste.

36 bxa3

As he played this move, Short offered a **draw** which Kasparov accepted immediately. If anything, after 36...♖xa3, Black has the better of it as the pawn on c3 is weak, and the bishop slightly loose, though the world champion saw no reason to prolong the match for no tangible reward.

The final score: Kasparov 12½ – Short 7½.